Relax in Retirement

Other Books by Kevin Guttman

The Swiss Army Knife of Retirement Cash Flow: Stories of Freedom & Assurance to Put Your Mind at Ease

****

Retire with Freedom & Confidence: Insights from Colorado Springs experts on living the lifestyle YOU DESERVE

Relax in RETIREMENT

Conversations with Denver Professionals on Maximizing Your Sunset Years

KEVIN A. GUTTMAN, M.A.

Sale of this book without a front cover may be unauthorized. If this book is coverless, it may have been reported to the publisher as "unsold or destroyed" and neither the author nor the publisher has received payment for it.

No part of this publication may be reproduced, stored in a retrieval system, or transmitted in any form or by any means, electronic, mechanical, photocopying, recording, or otherwise, without the prior written permission of the Publisher. Requests to the Publisher for permission should be sent to BMD Publishing, 5888 Main Street, Williamsville, NY 14221.

BMDPublishing@MarketDominationLLC.com
MarketDominationLLC.com

BMD Publishing CEO: Seth Greene
Editorial Management: Bruce Corris
Technical Editor, Cover Art & Layout: Kristin Watt

Copyright © 2018 Kevin Guttman
BMD Publishing
All Rights Reserved
ISBN # 978-1979341042

Printed in the United States of America

Every situation is unique. This book does not constitute financial or tax advice. Any resemblance to people mentioned is merely coincidental, etc. Please consult a financial advisor or tax advisor regarding your specific situation. Reverse mortgage borrowers are required to obtain a counseling certificate by attending a one-hour counseling session with a HUD-approved agency. At least one borrower must be at least 62 years old. This is not an offer to enter into an agreement. Not all customers will qualify. Information, rates and programs are subject to change without notice. All products are subject to underwriting and property approval. Other restrictions and limitations may apply.

DEDICATION

To all the professionals who serve seniors and their children,
thank you for your service!

ACKNOWLEDGMENTS

I am where I am today because of my family. My parents taught me to honor my elders, for which I am grateful. My wife Sabrena and children, Rachel, Garrett and Janee, Anna, Natalie and Abigail make life worth living. Thank you for all of your encouragement and support.

This book wouldn't have been possible without the help from the Market Domination LLC team. I am grateful to them for their dedication and hard work.

I want to thank every teacher, coach and counselor I have ever had. You made a difference and I am grateful.

I'm thankful for the many seniors who entered my life as reverse mortgage clients, and stayed as friends. I've learned much from you.

This book is dedicated to the hard-working, freedom-loving, God-fearing, senior American homeowners who still have dreams they want to live out and a legacy they want to leave for their families. May this book give you hope and show you that it's possible.

The idea behind this book was to interview top professionals from different industries who serve seniors who are approaching retirement or already retired. As the interviews were conducted, I was blown away by the expertise these people shared, and the care they have for seniors.

This book is chock-full of nuggets seniors and their families can use regarding taxes, real estate, Medicare, long-term care insurance, estate planning and elder care law. Because no matter what your age, too often people aren't even aware of the benefits available to them or how to access them.

The contributors to this book are at the top of their profession. I am grateful for their wisdom, insights and willingness to share their knowledge from years of experience with seniors in our community. My hope is that you will use the information in this book, and reach out to these caring advocates so that you can enjoy your golden years.

TABLE OF CONTENTS

ACKNOWLEDGMENTS vii
CHAPTER 1: Meet Kevin Guttman 1
CHAPTER 2: Scott Sparks, Financial Planner 11
CHAPTER 3: Pamela Meyer, Realtor-SRES 31
CHAPTER 4: Martha Hartney, Elder Care Attorney 47
CHAPTER 5: Aaron Eisenach, Long-Term Care Insurance 61
CHAPTER 6: Shawn Witkowski, EA CPS 83
CHAPTER 7: Ken Perrin, Financial Planner 95
CHAPTER 8: Carol Gosselin, Medicare Rep 111
CHAPTER 9: Anne McMichael, Estate Planning Attorney 125
CHAPTER 10: John Diak, Financial Planner 129
CHAPTER 11: Rick Sutton, Long-Term Care Insurance 145
CHAPTER 12: Kathy Chapman, Medicare Rep 157
CHAPTER 13: Cory Davern, Financial Planner 171
CHAPTER 14: Carolyn Brent, Senior Advocate 201
CHAPTER 15: Chris Mitchell, Life Insurance 221
CHAPTER 16: Michael Clark, Actuary 229
CLOSING THOUGHTS 251

CHAPTER 1

Meet Kevin Guttman

Before you hear from all the experts who were so willing to share valuable insights and information, I'd like you to hear from me. Who is Kevin Guttman? How did I get to this point in my life and my career? Why am I the one doing this book? And how did I develop such a passion for helping senior citizens live the retirement lifestyle they deserve?

I've been around real estate most of my life. You could say it's in my blood. My parents were in real estate. They were realtors, and they invested in properties. They flipped homes long before that's what it was called. As a little boy, I used to go with my dad to look at properties he was considering buying. I learned very young all about "location, location, location." Don't buy a house on a street with a double yellow line. Buy near schools, parks and shopping. Buy in good areas where people want to live. Always buy a three bed, two bath or bigger. Most important, buy the cheapest house in the best neighborhood.

When I got older, my brother and I worked for our dad, fixing up the homes. So, I learned a lot about home renovation, and how to get the most out of your investment. We were able to help him get some big increases in value with minimal investment.

Since my parents were both realtors, many nights that was the topic of conversation at the dinner table. We talked about the transactions they were working on, the clients they were helping, and all the different people they were working with—lenders, home inspectors, other realtors, and so on. It was a great education. Just hearing all those stories over the years gave me a real understanding of real estate—how it works, how important it is to people, and how it's such a key investment.

But I didn't go right into real estate as my career. I took a very roundabout path to get here. It was a path that took me around the world. When I first graduated from grad school, I joined a non-profit. It was an organization that helped people in very poor parts of the world. We helped them have clean water, schools for their children, medical clinics, and micro-enterprise business loans. I traveled throughout the country to raise money for these projects. And I was fortunate enough to travel around the world to see the work these people were doing. I counted it up the other day; I've been to 40 countries.

Growing up in America, we have no idea how poor some people are. Many have just one meal a day, and that one's not very filling. The lack of clean water. The lack of medical care. It was a very humbling experience. Millions and millions of people, more than a third of the developing world, live that way. So, knowing how much we were helping them was incredibly satisfying.

Of course, it's also not the best-paying work. And after a certain point, I knew I had to leave that position and do something else. By then, my wife and I had our five children, and it was getting harder and harder to support my family. Plus, the travel was getting difficult. I was gone half the time.

Let me tell you a little about my family. My wife Sabrena and I met in college and have been married since 1988. We have four daughters and a son, all born in the '90s. I'm very fortunate, because we're all very close and connected. We look out for each other and help each other and cheer each other on. The kids are all on very different and interesting career paths. One is starting a business. One is training to be a firefighter and another is studying to be an aircraft mechanic. The fourth wants to start her own women's clothing line, and our youngest wants to be a chef. Despite my background, no one is pursuing real estate—at least not yet.

But as I said, real estate is in my blood. When I left the non-profit world, I went into the profession I grew up in. At first, my wife and I followed in my dad's footsteps and started flipping homes. We enjoyed it, and made some money, but as many people know, it's a ton of work. And creating safe, affordable housing for people is very challenging. There's such a fine line between successfully flipping and really flopping. It is also extremely competitive.

I transitioned into the mortgage business in 2004. And I discovered it was a great way to help people. I enjoy educating people. And if you're doing mortgages the right way, a big part of the process is helping people understand their options in the biggest financial decision they'll make in their life. I enjoyed educating my clients and helping them make good choices. After the first year, I worked strictly by referral, and was getting plenty of new business. I was supporting my family and I was helping people. What a great combination.

Ironically, it was early in my new career that I first was exposed to reverse mortgages. Back in 2006, I went so far as to pursue training. But there were things about it that I wasn't sold on. I didn't think it was truly the best option for the client. So, I put it on the back burner and waited.

But, then, a few years ago, those things started to change. The FHA put in some new guidelines, and I liked the changes I saw. So, I went through training again in 2015, and discovered that it had changed a lot. The product improved and it was a better option for many people. I also found that I really enjoyed that age group. I like seniors. I like their values. I like what they stand for and I like who they are.

When I went through that training there were more than 100 people in my class with our company. Fewer than 10 percent are still doing reverse mortgages today. The fact is, they aren't easy to do. They can be very challenging. It's a different way of thinking, and involves a longer process to get the loans through. Because of their age and situation, and because this isn't as pressing as a mortgage for buying a home, the clients tend to take more time. They tend to need more time to think about it and process it. They want to talk to their kids, their friends or their advisors. That can be frustrating for some of my colleagues. But I don't mind. I just work with people at the pace that's comfortable for them.

And again, education is a big part of it. There's a lot of misinformation out there surrounding reverse mortgages, so it's important to make sure people know the facts, and see just how this can make their lives and retirement better.

I think that's really why I'm drawn to it; I truly feel I'm making a difference for people. I think about one client in particular—an elderly woman who had been referred to me by her daughter. I sat with her and got to know her a little, and I asked her, "Why do you want to do this? How can this help you?" She said, "Well, I have a duplex. I live on one side and I rent out the other. I'm 84 years old, I live by myself, and I still have a mortgage payment. It sure would be good if I didn't have that." I asked her about her budget and her cash flow situation. Her answer stunned me. She said, "To be honest, I have to use credit cards to buy food." All she had for income was Social Security and the rental income from the other half of the duplex. Once she paid her mortgage, she didn't have much left. So, we got her a reverse mortgage, which eliminated her mortgage payment and provided her the monthly cash flow she badly needed. She was able to pay off her credit cards and is now living comfortably. Imagine, she owned rental property, but she was barely treading water. Alleviating the pressure of her monthly mortgage payment was a game changer for her.

Another woman came to me and said, "My dad just died. I've moved in with my mother, because she has dementia and I need to take care of her. I hope Mom can stay in her home, but I'm not sure we can afford it." When her father died, his Social Security went away. They didn't have enough money to live on. So, we closed that loan and eliminated the mortgage payment. Now they can stay in the home.

Stories like that reinforce why I do this. Some seniors get a reverse mortgage to buy a second home or travel; but for many, this just makes a real difference in their lives. It lets them live the lifestyle they need and age in place without worrying about how to pay for it.

Many times, when a senior citizen comes into my office, I say, "Ma'am, it's not easy getting old; this getting old stuff just isn't for the faint of heart." They have all kinds of health issues and challenges. They're afraid of prices going up, and they're on a fixed income. They have all this uncertainty surrounding them. This is a way that we can just help them sleep better at night. In fact, I've had clients tell me just that. Just recently, I closed a loan for a woman and she said, "Do you know what this has done for me? I can sleep at night. I don't have to worry about money any more. I don't have to worry about this mortgage payment anymore." We always tell people, "As long as you maintain the home, live in it six months or more a year, and pay the property taxes and homeowner's insurance, you won't have a monthly mortgage payment. A mortgage payment is optional. You don't have to have one. That's a big deal for a senior to have that gone.

Let me tell one last story. I helped a couple buy a home last December. They were moving back to Colorado from Arkansas to be near their family. The husband was on oxygen. He didn't look bad, but he wasn't doing well. Two weeks ago, she called me up and said, "Do you remember me?" I said, "Of course." She said, "Well, my husband just died two weeks ago. Now, you told us as long as we live in the house, maintain it, pay the property tax and insurance, we won't have a mortgage payment. Is that right?" I said, "Yes, Ma'am." She said, "Well, I've got this statement," because every month a mortgage service center sends a statement. She said, "Can I bring this statement in and have you help me understand it?" I said, "Sure." She came in and we went through it and I made sure she understood how to read it. Afterward, she said, "I just need to let you know, the only way I can afford to live in my house is to not have a mortgage payment and you have no idea how much you've helped us." When I hear stories like that, I just say, "Wow, I really am helping people." It's very rewarding. It's very satisfying.

I know with regular mortgages you help people, but it seems the traditional mortgage market has been reduced to rates and fees. But, there's so much more to helping people get a loan than rates and fees, that reducing it to those factors alone kind of cheapens it. It's like Geico—15 minutes will save you 15 percent or more. There's a lot more to insurance than that. The same with mortgages. What you see online isn't necessarily all there is to it. Doing reverse mortgages suits me well because my clients seem to actually want to sit down and have a conversation. They want to get to know you, and you want to get to know them. I like that. I like knowing my clients and I like understanding their situation and what's going on with their family and how we can help them. I really like it a lot.

I also like the fact that it's a very challenging industry. Trying to explain a complex transaction like this to people—it's like reverse thinking. They don't naturally think this way. That's challenging.

The other thing that's difficult with it is that there are a lot of misperceptions out there. Some are outdated, some are just wrong. A lot of people just get something stuck in their mind, and it's tough to overcome. For example, the number one question people ask me is, "I have to turn my house over to the lender, right?" The answer, of course, is, "No, that doesn't happen. That never happens." The homeowner remains on title the whole time.

There are all these things people believe that aren't true. Many won't even take the time to learn the reality. And if they are willing to take the time, it can be an uphill climb to get them to learn and understand this product. Again, it's a challenge I enjoy taking on, because it's worth it in the end. There are so many misconceptions about reverse mortgages. I'll clear them up for you later in this book.

We often refer to a reverse mortgage as a Swiss Army Knife type of financial tool because it does so many things. It increases cash flow and eliminates a monthly mortgage payment. It can help pay for medical costs or for long-term care. It can help somebody fulfill a lifelong dream. It can help them leave a legacy for their family. We see people pull money out to buy a second home or vacation home and they don't have a mortgage payment on either house. There are so many different ways the proceeds can be used.

It's been known as a loan of last resort. But now we're seeing wealthy people take advantage of it. Let me tell you about a man who was in my office a few months ago. He told me that he had paid off his house, which was worth $400,000. I congratulated him; not everyone has done that. But then I said, "Let me ask you. What's the return of investment on your equity?" He told me about how the house had appreciated in value. I said, "No, I am asking about the equity. What's your return on your investment?"

He thought about it for a minute, and then said, "Zero." That's the point. Some people are okay with that. They don't want a mortgage payment. But this man knows how to leverage money, and this realization just ate away at him. He came back and said, "I want to put my money to work for me."

This was a man looking to get the most out of his assets. For many other seniors, the biggest issue they face during retirement is uncertainty. "How long am I going to live? What's the quality of my life going to be?" and "Do I have enough money?" They worry about inflation. They worry about their medical costs going up. They worry about the type of care they'll need as they get older. For many people, retirement is the perfect storm of financial uncertainty. They're on a limited income and they're spending down their savings. In many cases, the amount going out is a lot larger than the amount coming in. These circumstances weigh heavily on them. When we can alleviate some of the pressure, it's a life changer. It brings me such joy when they realize that that problem is no longer hanging over them.

That's why I'm writing this book—to help change lives. The professionals I've interviewed, such as financial planners, attorneys, CPAs, and insurance people, work with seniors on a regular basis. They're sharing their knowledge and experience. They're sharing the ideas they've had and the tools they've used. This book is a wonderful resource guide for seniors, those who are retired and those who are approaching retirement. It's also valuable for their kids. Because as our parents get older, roles get reversed. Throughout our lives, our parents are the ones we turn to for answers. For many seniors, this is the time they go to their kids and say, "What do you think of this?"

I can tell you, you'll learn so much from these interviews. I know I did. In addition to all the expertise they shared, I learned there are a lot of great people in our city who care deeply about seniors and want to do the right thing for them. They want to make sure our seniors are not taken advantage of. Some don't even care if they get paid. They just want to make sure these people are served well. It's very comforting to know that.

There are many resources for people, but they don't know about them. This book will help guide you to them. You can imagine how frustrating it is to talk to someone who can't help you, or you don't feel comfortable with that person, or sometimes you just don't trust them. The people in this book are the ones you can trust. They're experts in their field, and they want to do the right thing.

Whoever reads this book is tapping into all this brainpower. You're getting the knowledge you need to take advantage of different resources and make better decisions. So, let's get started!

CHAPTER 2

Scott Sparks

Scott Sparks is the founder and CEO of Sparks Financial, a Denver-based wealth management advisory firm serving 350 affluent, multi-generational families throughout the United States. With over a half billion serviced assets under management, Sparks Financial specializes in retirement distribution planning by balancing the art and science of the wealth accumulation and distribution phases in their clients' lives. Scott is known for developing highly-customized solutions for clients by applying holistic planning to calculate the risks and guide the investments associated with retirement and legacy planning.

A third-generation Coloradoan, Scott graduated from Colorado State University with a business administration degree in finance. He has also been featured as a contributor to the **Wall Street Journal, Forbes, Fortune, Money, Bloomberg and the Denver Business Journal**. He was named a **Financial Times** Top 400 Financial Advisors for 2017. Scott is active in the community. He serves as a member of the Children's Hospital Colorado Corporate Leadership Council and the Colorado State University Stadium Board. Scott and his wife Holli, live in Centennial, Colorado, where they enjoy skiing, hiking and fly fishing. To learn more about Sparks Financial, visit sparks-financial.com.

Kevin: I'm with Scott Sparks with Northwestern Mutual Insurance. We like to start off just trying to learn about where you're from and how you got here. Where did you grow up?

Scott: I'm a third generation Coloradoan, believe it or not. There aren't many of us. I grew up in the Lakewood area, went on to CSU in Fort Collins, and came back to Denver. I have not strayed much farther than 70 miles from here. This is home.

Kevin: Tell us about your childhood. What was it like? What did your parents do?

Scott: My dad was a teacher, then a principal, and also got into real estate. He was very involved in rental real estate. We had a number of units, so growing up, my life was filled with sporting events, school, and fixing rental properties.

Kevin: You and I have something in common. My parents were realtors and investors in Southern California. When there was a vacancy, my brother and I got that house ready for the next tenants.

Scott: It's hard work.

Kevin: It is hard work. What made you want to pursue a career in financial planning?

Scott: When I was in college, I gravitated to the financial industry in that I enjoyed math, enjoyed money, and enjoyed helping people. I was fortunate enough to do an internship with Northwestern Mutual my senior year, which got me exposed to the industry. So, it was just a passion for wanting to make a difference with people. I enjoyed numbers and dollars and planning and all the things that we do today.

Kevin: Northwestern Mutual is one of the top companies, according to publications that rank best companies to work for. It's always way up there.

Scott: What I like about my situation is I'm essentially independent and choosing to affiliate with Northwestern Mutual. We've had the privilege of being interviewed by a number of other firms that really wanted my firm to move to their organization, so that allowed us to do a lot of due diligence on other firms that are out there in our space. After lots and lots of due diligence, I think our clients are best served here, if you want the truth. Plus, the fact that we serve as a fiduciary on our advisory accounts, which is a dramatically different environment today than it once was.

Kevin: No kidding. Scott, what do you wish you had known when you started that you know now?

Scott: I think what I wish I would have known is that our industry has a lot of complexity, and I wish I would have been smart enough to know that I needed to surround myself with smarter people sooner. I was a little slow at that. If I had it to do over, I would have involved more people in my organization at an earlier age and an earlier stage. Today, I know that I don't know everything, nor will I ever know everything about anything.

This industry has a lot of complexity. I feel for the end consumers because they're bombarded with all kinds of strategies and ideas and trying to win now. That's why I've involved a number of people on our team. They are very smart and have a lot of expertise in this area. We've strategically built our team with different people that have strengths in different areas.

Kevin: That's awesome. How long have you been with Northwestern Mutual?

Scott: I've been in the industry now 29 years. We have about 160 years of collective team experience. I run a team of 13 people..

Kevin: What are the lines of products that you tend to offer your clients?

Scott: We really come at it from a planning approach. I would say we're planning-focused, not product-focused. There are situations where we get involved with a client where we're purely in planning and engagement, serving as a fiduciary, presenting and executing on a financial analytical plan. Then there may be investment solutions on the backend that help carry out that plan that we can be engaged with. That's another engagement entirely.

In that space, it's investment management, so we manage a lot of money for clients. We like the fact that Northwestern Mutual is an independent broker dealer, so they don't manufacture any investment product in the investment space that we get paid more to sell. A lot of firms out there are still not true fiduciaries in that sense. They have manufactured products where they may be charging a fee on assets under management, but they're also getting paid a fee to place their own product. We like the fact that we can have open architecture, and whether we want to use Vanguard or some other solution, we're looking for the best end result. Investment management is part of it. Insurance is another component. We're one of about 5,000 teams in the country that get access to Northwestern Mutual products, but we have access to investments and different insurance carriers for situations where Northwestern Mutual isn't a good fit, or where the client can't medically qualify.

Kevin: It's really the best of both worlds, and you're not locked in with certain products.

Scott: It really is. It's the planning coupled with a personalized solution that gets the client to the end game. It's wide-open architecture. It's the best avenue I've seen in my 29-year career of helping us get on the same side of the table as the client, and truly working on something that's advantageous for everybody.

Kevin: I'm a client of Northwestern Mutual myself. One of the reasons I like the company is that it's a mutual company. Can you explain why that's important?

Scott: I think the insurance industry is perceived as focusing on making money. The National Association of Insurance Commissioners notes that non-mutual companies accounted for an overwhelming majority of the overall U.S. insurance industry in 2013, with mutual companies holding less than 18 percent of total U.S. insurance industry cash and invested assets[1]. The people that make money in those institutions are the stockholders, people who buy stock in them, not necessarily the insurance policy holders.

Kevin: That means every year or quarter, however they pay, the policyholders get a dividend. Is that right?

Scott: Policyholders may receive a dividend, which can go toward paying premiums, purchasing additional insurance, or taking the payment in cash. It's far more

---

[1] http://www.naic.org/capital_markets_archive/150428.htm

efficient than what most people see in the industry, which are the other types of companies.

Kevin: This book is geared primarily to seniors and their kids. I know you help people of all ages, but are there specific ways that you help seniors?

Scott: Well, we really have an area of expertise in retirement distribution planning. That is helping people get through this era where we're largely seeing the first generation in history retiring without a pension. My grandfather worked for the Denver Water Board for 42 years. With his pension and Social Security, he pretty much had the same paycheck in retirement that he had while working. That is not the era of people retiring today. They're trying to figure out how they get from 65 to conceivably a hundred years old without a predictable paycheck. Our firm really has specialized in thinking about how we do that efficiently, how we decrease risk, how we increase probability of success and how we optimize their balance sheet for what they've built and spent their life's work doing, so that they can pull the trigger, retire, and live comfortably and not worry.

Kevin: The phases are accumulation, preservation, and distribution. Is that right?

Scott: Correct. As we think about that, distribution can mean lots of things. Our clients tend to want to not run out of their money during their lifetime, but they also have a desire, many of them at some level, to leave something behind. Trying to do that in the most efficient way possible is really, really important—making sure we roll that balance sheet through time in the most efficient way possible.

Kevin: You're looking at all kinds of things. You're looking at their income, their lifestyle, the tax burden—all of it from a comprehensive point of view.

Scott: We're looking at it in a real comprehensive point of view. We believe in a team approach. We work with their accountant, their attorney, and other family members, to have more input on their situation and make sure there are no blind spots.

Kevin: It's important that you say comprehensive, because leaving out just one of those things could really sideswipe them, or wipe them out, or ultimately be bad for their estate.

Scott: You're right. The worry that most people have is they don't know what they don't know, and so that's our objective. We're fortunate to have a lot of intuitive people here. We have a lot of expertise and we have a lot of people that we can go to through the Northwestern Mutual system as well. But, we also have the privilege of having clients, in many cases, that are 10, 20, in some cases, 30 or 40 years down the road from where our current clients are. So, we have the benefit of learning from their hindsight and giving our clients some foresight to help make sure they don't make mistakes.

Kevin: That's important. What are the highlights of your role, Scott?

Scott: The highlights of my role, in all honesty, are helping people bring complexities down to something they understand, and bringing peace of mind to people. Our firm's mission statement is helping people define, build, and enjoy prosperous lives. Prosperity doesn't necessarily mean more money. It's helping people clearly define what they want. What they want financially, but more important, what they want for themselves personally, and professionally, if they're going to continue to work part-time. It's trying to make the life that they want come to fruition.

Kevin: One of the things we see with seniors is that they want to stay at home as long as they can. What are some things that you do to advise them so they can age in place and stay at home?

Scott: One of the risks that has been uncovered by some of the smartest minds in finance, is that not only are we losing pension and other income streams, but people are living longer and, in many cases, in the tail end of their life their health starts to fail. That can be tremendously expensive. My grandmother suffered from Alzheimer's disease for 13 years, and it financially devastated her.

Yet, people do want to stay in their own home as long as possible. That's their desire. It's developing a game plan around, "What does that look like if, in fact, that happens?" Part of our practice is helping people do risk management. "Is that something where we need to set aside certain funds for that event? Do we offload some of that risk to an insurance company?" We help them explore their options.

Kevin: What are some of the most common mistakes you see seniors make as they approach or are in retirement?

Scott: I think the biggest mistake I see people make as seniors, as they approach, and during retirement for sure, is they try and go at it alone. The reality is, investment management in particular is an emotional situation, and when you're doing it yourself with your own money, the biggest mistake I see people make is they do the wrong thing at the wrong time. We manage our clients' assets with a very disciplined process. For example, our advisory accounts have an investment policy statement that helps keep everybody on the same page, and as market movements go up and down they don't make people freak out and do the wrong thing at the wrong time.

Kevin: That's inevitable, isn't it? The market is going to go up and down, for who knows how long? That's just what happens.

Scott: Right. Markets go up and down, and as we see our clients get older and quit working, they see those ups and downs as more pronounced. They also have more time to think about it and worry about it. Consequently, I think having somebody that helps guide them down the path is really important.

Kevin: How do you help the seniors solve these problems?

Scott: Well, we help them develop a strategy and a philosophy around that. We identify dollars for different windows of time. For instance, dollars they need over the next three years don't need to be on the rollercoaster of the market. We don't want any market risk. We want to have dollars allocated to time frames and allocated to certain risk categories that make sense. We believe in a base income first strategy, meaning every client we work with has some sort of level of income that they "need." They have another level of income above that, that they "want," travel, or whatever that might be. So, we really clearly define income strategies to meet that needed level, and investment strategies to meet what's above that. That gives them the peace of mind, that they can live a comfortable life. The biggest mistake I think that seniors make is they end up letting their investment plan dictate their life plan, not their life plan dictate their investment plan.

Kevin: Well said. One of the things I tell people when I meet with them is it's really about cash flow in retirement, isn't it? That's the bottom line.

Scott: It is. You know, people that lived 30 or 40 years—depending on how long they worked—on a paycheck, surrounded their life around that paycheck, and all of a sudden, they no longer have a paycheck. The more we can recreate a paycheck in retirement, the happier they are, and the better investors they are. It just works better.

Kevin: Yes. Scott, what do you like best about your business?

Scott: What I like best about our business is we have the ability to impact people in every single meeting. We have the ability to bring some intelligence to them, or identify something that maybe they were not previously aware of. So that impact is helpful. Sometimes that's very rewarding. Joyful situations like people retiring, celebrating that, sending them paychecks, or sending their kids to college. In some cases, it's other situations where they have an illness or an injury or they pass away prematurely. In all aspects, there are things that we need to plan for, but clearly, impact is number one.

Kevin: That's interesting. As you go through life, sometimes these things happen that you didn't think would ever happen to you.

Scott: And I think it's comforting having the amount of experience we have at the firm, so we can tell our clients, "You're not the first this has happened to." It's comforting for them to know that everybody thinks their life may have a bad turn, but the reality is we get to see it all the time. We see public Facebook pictures and all those things, all the joyful things that happen to people. But, behind every great story is another story that probably isn't being told.

Kevin: Absolutely. Is there a product, technique, or service that you offer you wish more of your senior clients knew about?

Scott: I think the service and the ability is really just the second opinion, the ability for people to sit down with somebody else and give them a second opinion on their situation. We meet a lot of people that are in their 50s and 60s that have worked with other advisors. Those advisors have been really good. There are a lot of very smart people in the business. But, the people that sometimes got you through the accumulation phase probably haven't spent as much time as we have in the distribution phase. So, what we find is just that ability to have a second opinion, worst-case scenario, makes people feel good about what they're already doing. If we come back and identify that everything's right on track, that feels good to a client. However, there may be one or two things we uncover that could have a significant impact, possibly to the next generation, tax-wise or otherwise. Really, that ability to get a second opinion, I think, gives those people peace of mind and comfort to exit and go into retirement with confidence, and that confidence is what makes that more fun, I think.

Kevin: Is it safe to say that the skill set and the knowledge that somebody in the accumulation phase has is different than the distribution phase?

Scott: Absolutely. I think, for every person we've had retire, we see three things happen. First, they get more conservative that day. Second, almost every one of them hates paying taxes more in retirement than they ever did working. I haven't met anybody that loves paying taxes, but when you're working, you get to pay your taxes out of the paycheck. When you pay your taxes in retirement, you have to pay it out of your asset base and your nest eggs. That just feels not as good. Then, third, as people get older they want more simplicity, not complexity. Studies show that the average person might go from seven advisors to three. Being able to accomplish all three of those things and knowing that we see that on a reoccurring basis with all of our clients is advantageous for us in helping our clients that are younger than that position themselves to know that's going to happen.

Kevin: Scott, think about a recent client that you helped, a senior client. We don't want to know their name or anything like that, but what was the situation? What did they hope to accomplish? And how did you help them?

Scott: We had a client who came to us recently who was contemplating retirement within a year. He was also managing his mother's asset base and trying to make that hold up throughout her lifetime. Her health was starting to fail. He was feeling a bit overwhelmed. He had done a lot of it on his own. He had a retirement plan through his employer. It all was feeling like it was crashing in on him.

So, he went through a number of interviews. He interviewed five financial advisory firms and came in with a laundry list of questions. It was a very good experience in the sense that he was doing his due diligence. I'm happy to say that at the end of that process, he selected us to be his advisor. We just did a review with him, a second annual review, and he expressed to us the comfort of being able to address all the different components back to that holistic, comprehensive planning approach, both including his situation and his mom's. It really was helpful to him, and he was excited to hear that he was going to make it, she was going to make it, and everybody was on track.

He also said he appreciated our honesty in bringing up some of the less exciting things that he hadn't thought about in terms of some of the risks. We have a very good, open dialogue and relationship. As he puts it, we're one of his number one favorite trusted advisors, and that feels good to know. He's actually on a bike ride in Europe, and enjoying his life, doing what he planned for 40 years to do. That feels good to us as well.

Kevin: Is it safe to say that you talk about the things that people don't like to talk about? We don't want to think about death. We don't want to think about getting disabled and not being able to work, long-term care, those kinds of things. Is that just human nature?

Scott: Yes, I think human nature is that we don't like to go there. There are also people who have had experiences with people in the investment and/or the insurance industry that have positioned some of those ideas in a very negative light. People, in general, might not have had great experiences with advisors talking about that in the right light. But the truth of the matter is, as a good advisor holistically looking out, we need to make sure that we're uncovering all risks and identifying all opportunities, all threats. It's something that's important. I think in our industry it's critically important to make sure that it's the right fit. The client likes the advisor and the advisor likes the client.

We've also strategically built our firm so that we have multi-generational structure in-house. We work with clients that are second- and third-generation families. They want to know that if the bus, for instance, hits Scott that we have an entire team of people that know their situation. We have a written out, documented, funded succession agreement internally. A 2012 Cerulli study showed that 70 percent of advisors 60 and older are sole proprietors, and 75 percent of them do not have a succession plan[2]. Having that foresight to plan for them, just like they hopefully did for their business, is important for us to do, because we take it very seriously.

Kevin: I have to say, I think a client would think, "Man, these people are serious. They're going to have my best interests at heart." Who's an ideal client for you?

Scott: Our firm has a lot of capacity and a lot of opportunity. We're fortunate to work with a lot of folks all over the country. We really have two ideal clients that we help. One would be that older client, generally 50-plus. They've done a good job of accumulating wealth. Generally, net worth is five million or more. They have a lot of assets. They have more complexity and more needs in that space. That really brings our whole team into that equation.

---

[2] http://www.investmentnews.com/article/20140203/FREE/140209995/one-third-of-advisers-plan-to-exit-business-within-a-decade

We have a second group of people that we call our emerging affluent clients. Those might be people in their 20s making a couple hundred thousand dollars as a household, in their 30s making three hundred thousand or more as a household, or in their 40s making four hundred thousand. Maybe they haven't built the wealth up yet, but they're on a good track and they're keeping a good eye, but they're really, really busy. They value advice and they're good stewards of their money, but they're busy.

Those two groups of people are the groups we add. We might add 15 to 20 people in each of those categories in a year. We don't decide to work with everybody, and not everybody decides to work with us. So, we want to make sure it's a fit. We want to make sure it's a cultural fit. What we aren't, is a stock trading, stock picking firm. We aren't going to be seeing around corners. We don't have crystal balls. We don't have some of the things that some people want us to have. So, we want to make sure it's a good fit for both parties.

Kevin: That's great. With these ideal clients, what would be the first step you'd want them to take?

Scott: For us, the first step is really just getting an assessment. It's getting to know what their goals and objectives are. It's a very in-depth, fact-finding process of assessing where they are today, and starting to develop a blueprint of where they want to go and how might we do that. As we get more and more data from the potential client, we involve more and more of our team to really come in and give a second opinion, develop analytics around the planning that they want to accomplish, and start to identify the place of most potential and the place of most threat.

Kevin: How do you currently market to these ideal clients to help them know about you and your firm?

Scott: Historically, we do a lot of work within the national system of Northwestern Mutual. There are a lot of folks in the Northwestern Mutual system. Maybe other advisors have a concentration in insurance only. We happen to be one of the largest teams in the country with Northwestern Mutual, doing more of the distribution, investment management, comprehensive planning approach. We have a lot of connection in that space. Number two, we have a lot of great clients that are raving fans of what we do. They tell their friends about what we do, and so we get a lot of introductions from existing clients.

Kevin: It's beautiful. What's the biggest challenge you're facing right now?

Scott: I think the biggest challenge that we're facing is making sure that as our clients go down that distribution path, or start to position themselves for the distribution path, that we really do have a good handle on what they are going to be spending. I think a lot of people don't completely understand what they're going to be spending in retirement. So, we do spend a lot more time on that. What we've experienced, is that in the first five years of retirement people tend to spend a bit more than they anticipated. If you think about your life, on Saturday and Sunday we spend more money than we do on Monday, Tuesday, Wednesday, and Thursday. When every day's Saturday, people tend to spend more money. It's trying to make sure that we have a good, solid process around them, identifying what their wants and their needs in income mean.

Kevin: What's the best advice you've ever received?

Scott: I think the best advice that we've received is, "Listen more than you talk when you're sitting in front of a client." I think the biggest mistake our industry makes is that we jump to conclusions. Not every client's the same. Not every client wants the same thing. The biggest, best advice is listen and ask good questions. Always, always, always, our number one rule in our firm is do the right thing for the client no matter what happens.

Kevin: That's a good way to live. What would you like to share that I haven't asked you?

Scott: You've asked a lot of great questions. I don't know that there's anything dramatically different. I do think the second-opinion situation, especially for people that are 50-plus, has really served us well. It's served our potential clients—who in many cases become clients—well.

Having that certainty, it's like getting diagnosed with some major disease. Most people don't take the first advice they get from the first doctor. They want to go to the second doctor. In many cases, they find a better solution the second time around. I think we're seeing that people have a lot of fear around this subject matter. How do we create an environment that creates less fear? Going through our process, again, does not mean every single person becomes a client. But we'll be honest with them and tell them where their blind spots might be. They can go back and either implement with their current person or someone other than us, but not one person, in years, has gone through our process and said it was a complete waste of time.

Kevin: This fear, is it fear of the unknown? Is it fear because I don't want to feel stupid or because I don't know much about finance? What's behind the fear, do you think?

Scott: I think the fear is, "I don't know what I don't know and I read all these crazy things about everything." To the consumer, one of the challenges is, with media the way it is today, there's such access to information. I think about my kids. When I used to have a question when I was a kid, I might have to go to the library to look it up. But they can look it up in about 42 seconds. At the same time, when it comes to this subject matter, you can read 10 articles that tell you to do one thing and 10 that tell you to do the exact opposite thing. It's the fear of which advice is the right advice. The fear is, "I don't want to have to go back to work at 75 years old. I don't want to run out of money. I don't want to make a mistake."

Kevin: I can't make a bad decision.

Scott: Yes. Everything's magnified in retirement. One of the things that we see is that when somebody's working and they're 50 years old and the 2008 market hits, in many cases that's an opportunity. They get to continue to invest in the markets. If you're 65 and just retired and that happens, you no longer get to out-earn your mistake, so to speak. That's a fear that I think is real.

We rely on academic research commissioned by Northwestern Mutual, coupled with real-world experience from our clients that are, in many cases, down the road from our current clients. What are they telling us they like? What are they telling us they wish they might have done earlier? Where that science meets real-world emotional feelings has been really extremely helpful to people.

Kevin: That's a great answer. Where can people go to learn more about you? How can they find you?

Scott: We're on social media. On Facebook, it's sparks-financial. Our website is http://www.sparks-financial.com/. We're on LinkedIn. We have a number of sites that you can get access to. Our local telephone number is 303-512-2123.

Kevin: Thank you, Scott.

CHAPTER 3

Pamela Meyer

Pamela Meyer is the real estate advisor at Denver Home Navigators, affiliated with Keller Williams Realty. She has worked in the Denver real estate industry for more than 25 years.

Pamela is also a Certified Senior Housing Professional and a Senior Real Estate Specialist. She helps seniors and others looking to downsize or *rightsize,* and provides a team of resources that helps seniors with later-in-life moves.

Pamela 's approach is built on personal touches, win-win deals and positive results. She uses the latest technologies, market research and business strategies to map out custom-tailored solutions for her clients, and works to make sure their moves leave them overjoyed, not overwhelmed.

Kevin: We're talking to Pamela Meyer, with Denver Home Navigators, which is a part of Keller Williams. Pamela, tell us a little about yourself. Where did you grow up?

Pamela: I actually grew up in the Denver metro area. But I'm not a native. My husband is, so sometimes I'm reminded that I'm not. I was five when we moved to the Denver metro area.

Kevin: So, you're almost a native.

Pamela: Almost. I've been here for a long time, since I've now broken the 60 marker. I got into real estate the first time when I was very young. I sold real estate for a year and left with my ego in shreds because I was in my early twenties. Sales in general is just tough. Then I taught realtors for 15 years with a multiple listing service. I got back into the business and re-licensed in 2002. And I have been doing residential real estate full time ever since. My focus in the last seven or eight years has been much more toward my own demographic, which are those of us, I say, 55 and better. I have my Senior Real Estate Specialist designation from NAR. I also have a certified Senior Housing Professional designation with a group that doesn't want to be associated with NAR because they don't want to offer any Continuing Education credits. They don't want people to take their class just to get CE credit. They want people who have a passion for working with seniors, and that's not for everybody.

Kevin: Agreed.

Pamela: You also have to have enough patience. I'll tell you, my clients can take six months to two or three years to pull the trigger. So, you have to be patient and ready to help them with resources along the way, because it's not a simple, "Hey, let's put a sign in the yard." At least in most cases, it's not.

Kevin: So, tell us about your childhood. What was it like?

Pamela: It was pretty easy going. My parents got married young. We lived back east and came out here when I was five, which was in 1960. I didn't know this at the time since I was only five, but the family members were warning my parents in all seriousness. They looked at them very seriously over their glasses and said, "You realize there are Indians out there." Like we were going to the Wild West, as far as the family was concerned on the east coast. I was born in Massachusetts. We lived in Philadelphia while my dad finished college, then lived in Greenwich, Connecticut, and then moved out here. He was a stockbroker and an old company called Bosworth Sullivan was opening an office out in the Wild West.

Kevin: Among the Indians.

Pamela: Among the Indians. I went to public schools here, and then I went to college here in two different locations. I went to CU Boulder for about two weeks, thought I was in love and wanted to get married, and left. Then I worked for a couple years and said, "Oh maybe I really do need to go to college," so I went down to Colorado Springs and went to Colorado College for a couple of years. Then I thought I wanted to get married again, but I promised myself I would finish my degree before I turned 30. And I kid you not, Kevin, I blinked my eyes and I was 28. "Oh, my gosh, I have two years to finish." So, I did. It was a University of Phoenix program to get my Bachelor of Science in Business Administration. As it turned out, I didn't end up using that. I went and got licensed as a realtor.

Kevin: So, what made you want to pursue real estate?

Pamela: My mother was a realtor. I tried it once very young, and then I tried it again when I was older. But I never really left the industry. I was teaching at Metrolist, our multiple listing service, from 1985 to 2002.

Kevin: What do you wish you had known then, that you know now?

Pamela: How you need to have a long-term approach to real estate. I tell people who are thinking about getting into the business to have six months of savings in the bank, because it isn't a salary position. You have to be ready, willing and able to deal with closings. Sometimes you have a bunch and sometimes you have nothing. So, you have to be disciplined, and not just go, "Woohoo! Got a big check!" and go spend it all. I pay myself a set amount every month and, with any luck, what's been the trick for me is to give myself a bonus at the end of the year. I've lived within the budget, and then I get a bonus.

Kevin: That's a great way to do it.

Pamela: Because you have business expenses that are ongoing regardless of whether or not you have a closing. You have to keep your face out there; you have to be interacting with people. The thing I did do though, from the start, was build my business on relationships. I didn't put my name on bus benches. I don't need my face on a grocery cart. Because the vast majority, over 90 percent of my business, is repeat and referral business. You know, with someone who knows someone, who they want to introduce me to.

Kevin: Me, too. And that's a great way to do business.

Pamela: It's a much better way than transaction-oriented, because then you only have that transaction. Someone said to me once, "You make me feel like I'm your only client. Even though I know I'm not, I feel like I am." I've always thought of that. I'm mindful to make my people feel like they're the only one because the truth of the matter is, if I do my best work for them, they are my best advertisements.

Kevin: I feel the same way, a hundred percent. So, how did you come to focus on helping seniors?

Pamela: Part of it was that I was in the demographic, of what I say, is 55 and better, not fifty-five and older. I also had the good fortune to be acquainted with a builder who was building a 55-plus community here in the metro area. I was what was called a "smart move realtor." So, if someone came in and didn't have an agent, I would help coordinate with the builder to get their property sold. And I would sell their property for less of a listing commission, and I'd get the buy side. It was a win-win for me, because although I was making less money selling their house, I didn't have to drive them all over town. We didn't have to hunt for four or five months to find the right place for them. If I did my best work for them, which I did just the same as if I had listed at full commission, then they knew people who would move. That's always my motto; they're going to know somebody.

For most of the people in my age group—I could record them time and time again and say almost unanimously—the words out of their mouths are, "I am never moving again." And the truth of the matter is, in our age group, one thing changes and we move. I have helped a number of people from that builder make the move. Because something either happens health-wise, they lose a spouse, they want to be closer to the grandkids, or they foresee something coming down the pike with regard to long-term health and they decide, "I really do need to be closer to family." Many of them will move into this community because it's in Highlands Ranch, and that's where their kids or grandkids live. But, even then, if you lose a spouse or something else isn't going the way you want it to health-wise, you need to make other decisions.

Kevin: You're right. Pamela, what are some of the highlights of your position?

Pamela: I was just telling somebody this the other day. I think that part of the highlight is who I get to work with, people that are very like-minded to myself. It may not be politically correct to say this, but the truth is, I'm a Christian. For the vast majority of us who are 55 and better, who were raised at a time in our history when the vast majority were Christians, that was normal. Also, we grew up in a time when if you shook hands on something, you did what you said you were going to do.

Kevin: A love for country and respect for authority.

Pamela: All of that. So, because my clients and I are so like-minded in so many ways, they become friends. It's a nice position to be in. We visit after closing. I have a client who just lost her husband in March. We go to lunch and I check in on her. Luckily, she has a really good community of friends in this development she moved into. I'm very happy for that. She knew that he would predecease her, she just didn't know when. But to have the desire to continue that relationship, beyond the transaction timeframe, is a real benefit. I enjoy it a lot.

Kevin: I'm right there with you. So much of what you're saying resonates with me as well. You know one of the big things with seniors is they want to age in place. They want to stay at home as long as they can. What are some ways you help them do that?

Pamela: For the most part, I have resources that I can put them in touch with to help adapt the home to meet their needs. I am not that expert, and I'm not the handyman, but I know them. There are some simple things I know. Remove rugs and make sure cords are out of the way. There's a lot of stuff you need to do. My own mother, who just passed away in June, was almost 82, but hadn't been in good health for a while. So, just removing any stumbling blocks, anything that can get in the way of them moving around safely is important. I have handymen who install grab bars, comfort height toilets, walk-in tubs—or pull out a tub altogether and just do a shower with a seat. People have different preferences. I'm ready to yank my own tub in my master bath, after I broke an ankle a couple years ago. It was just brutal. So, I see the reasoning for having walk-in, minimal steps, that kind of thing. I live in a two-story house now, and I think that it keeps me fit. Yet, if I were to move tomorrow, as fit as I am, I would move to a main floor living situation. I want to be in control of my move and not forced into a move—whether it be temporary or permanent—because I either need a hip or a knee.

And that's what most of my older clients are looking for. Most of my clients, the really forward-thinking ones, are doing this before they need to. And generally, most of us make smarter decisions when we are proactive rather than reactive. When you're reactive, quite frankly, people end up moving twice as often as you would like to believe. There's the reflex move like, "Oh, your hip's broken. We have to move." And then you move into an environment that doesn't support you and isn't where you want to stay long-term. There's also a lot of my age group that's helping their parents. So, whether it's the perspective of helping someone or doing it yourself, I call it *rightsizing* instead of downsizing, because downsizing makes you feel like you're losing something.

Kevin: I like that phrase, too.

Pamela: But also, helping with moving mom and dad. Sometimes the kids can't. The parent doesn't want to hear from the children because they still feel like the parent. So, "It's none of your business how much money I have, or what I want to do, it's my house." And you have to kind of tiptoe around that discussion to help begin the conversation of when. "What would you want to have happen if you couldn't live here? What would you want to do?"

Kevin: So, what are some of the most common mistakes you see seniors make as they approach or are in retirement?

Pamela: I would say the most prevalent mistake is thinking that they're going to do it all by themselves. I have people moving out of family homes or who need to move out of family homes, and I'm just as guilty. I've lived in my home for more than 20 years. Both my husband's parents and mine have passed away, and more stuff has come into our house than has left it. Most of us are dealing with too much stuff. And we think we're capable of going through it. But the truth of the matter is that we get into that storage room or that bedroom and we pick up one box and three hours later we're still on that box, because we get lost in the memories of the box. Whereas, I have some people that work a lot to help people de-clutter and organize. And they are not going to let anything leave the house that you haven't laid eyes on, and said, "That can go."

I think that's people's biggest fear in enlisting the help of someone else, because they think that somebody is going to get rid of something that they want to keep. And this particular group does not do that. They can pick up the boxes, they can empty the closets, and they can bring the stuff to you. If you're not very physically able to move around, you can sit. I have clients who sat down, and the organizers brought stuff in front of them and said "What about this? What about this? What about this?" A box of sweaters is easy to go through, it takes you two seconds. A box of papers is a whole lot different. I still enlist the help of an organizer, because I don't have a secretary.

I have a home office that takes care of my family's household stuff and my business. There's more paperwork than I want to deal with on a regular basis. So, I have someone help me. That's the biggest thing. People think they have to do it by themselves.

I have a couple now…some knee replacements got in the way and postponed their move, but they're still trying to do it themselves. I have another gentleman who's putting his house on the market next spring and he had me out this spring. We talked about what he should do and what he should not do, what he should spend money on and what he shouldn't spend money on. One of my organizers is going over to meet with him, because he is compromised physically. He needs to get stuff out of bookcases and closets, and stuff like that, to say, "Yes, no, donate." These organizers are worth every dime, because they keep you on track. You can get lost in the memories of that stuff you're not sure about later. We'll put that in the "I'm-not-sure" pile, and then you make a decision about it next time you meet. Because of the clutter they just will ignore it, and not deal with the

"We really should think about this." As I said, people who are willing to think about what moves they might want to make, should they need to, before a health crisis makes them move, make better and more financially wise decisions.

Kevin: So, it really is the proactive versus reactive. What do you like best about your business, Pamela?

Pamela: I think the people that I work with. You know, for me it's all about the relationships. The transaction generally is pretty easy going. Most of my clients, again because of the age group, have been disciplined with their money. Many of them own their homes outright, and they just want to be wise with what they're going to do with that. Very few of my clients, even if they're selling an $800,000 house, want to go reinvest all that money in anything. They want to take part of it and pay for something, and they want to take the rest of it and live on it, or augment their retirement. It's fun because, in most cases, they're not under stress. Although, selling your home is always stressful. I don't care how excited you are about doing it, it is stressful. So, my goal is to make that stress as short a period of time as possible.

Kevin: What product, technique or service do you offer that you wish more of your senior clients knew about?

Pamela: I think probably just my resources that help them get stuff done, that takes stuff off their plate. Does it cost money? Yes. But I will tell you that every client of mine who's ever used these organizers I'm talking about, every stinking one of them has said, "Oh my gosh! It was worth every dime and more!" because of how much more they were able to get done than when they were working on their own. As capable as we might be, it's just hard for us. We get lost in the stuff. So, just the number of resources between handymen, organizers, estate sale people, painters, and so on. There are all sorts of resources that most realtors have, but these are specifically geared toward people who are trying to get out of a house that has too much stuff.

Kevin: Tell us about a recent client. What were they hoping to accomplish? And how did you help them?

Pamela: I actually sold a property for a couple that was out of town. The husband has dementia; the wife does not. They had moved into a 55 and older community they thought they would be able to stay at. Their kids and grandkids are in California. And it became more and more apparent that it was important for them to relocate while they could. So not only did I list the property, get it on the market, and get it sold, but it was all long distance. She didn't come into town until it was closing time.

Kevin: So, you handled all of it?

Pamela: I just handled it all. They had a neighbor who was very helpful in picking up the mail and stuff like that, but they were out in California. And there was stuff happening in their lives out there that just made it difficult to come back here. Luckily, the house was pretty show ready. It was easy to get staged, have photos done, all that kind of stuff. I made a point of removing some items that were in plain sight that would just be an invitation to disappear while the property is on the market. So, I would send her little emails, "Okay, I put the laptop here, I took these watches and what looks to be like some more of your valuable jewelry and I put them over here. They're not in your jewelry area. Just so you know, if you come back while I'm not there, you'll know your stuff is still there."

Kevin: Tell us, who is an ideal client for you Pamela?

Pamela: I would say an ideal client is someone, certainly in this demographic, who is thinking ahead and says, "You know, it might not have to be tomorrow, but we're really thinking we want to *rightsize*. This is too much house and too much work." Some people, if they're really proactive, do it while they still have the energy to get some stuff done. They are wanting to travel and want "lock and leave" living. I had clients a few years ago who weren't even 60 yet. Their kids were grown and out of the house and they said, "Oh my goodness gracious! We are so glad we moved now, because we worry about what kind of energy we would've had to do this, even five years from now, let alone ten." So, they're really happy that they made that move. It was a little bit smaller square footage. They probably had about 3,200 square feet and moved into 2,700 square feet with a different layout and no maintenance, "lock-and-leave" living. So, when they travel they don't have to worry about snow, grass, mail or anything.

Kevin: With these ideal clients what's the first step you'd want them to take?

Pamela: Well, the first step is to meet me face-to-face. I prefer that to be in their home, so that I can see what their home is. I think this business is very important to do face-to-face. I've done a radio program and people hear things, but I think it's a different situation when you get eyeball-to-eyeball with somebody. I think most people have a pretty good sense of, "Can I trust this person or not? Do they walk their talk? Are they who they say they are?" I would venture to say that most people know who they're getting when they get me. I don't change a lot when I'm in realtor mode versus running around with my grandkids mode.

Meeting face-to-face is the important first step, because no one is committed. Both sides get a sense of, "Do I trust this person? Do we communicate well?" Communication is such a key ingredient to the whole situation. If we don't communicate well, then it's pointless to move ahead. I think the client has to feel like I get them, that I get what they want or need, and that I pay attention to what they're saying they want and need. I would say one of the biggest complaints I've heard from people is that they don't feel realtors listen to them. They told the realtor their max price was $400,000 and they were being shown $500,000 properties. Well, that's kind of stupid. I can safely say I don't care if you can afford a million-dollar house, my perimeters are what you say you're comfortable with, and if we don't find what you want, you'll be the one to tell me to up the price. Not me.

Kevin: What would you say is the biggest challenge you're facing right now?

Pamela: People who aren't sure where they would want to move, because the truth of the matter is, right now in 2017 we still have an inventory shortage. There's not enough inventory on the market now. Builders over the years haven't built as much product for the tsunami of those of us turning 65 every day for the next 18 years to really address what we are going to need. Ranch style homes, ranch style homes with casitas, duplexes. Something where someone could live next door to you, and you could still have your independence, but yet close to someone who could help you if you need it. Not everybody wants a 55 and older community. I would say that's not the biggest requirement I see. The next biggest requirement I see is main floor living, main floor bathroom, main floor master, and main floor laundry. You can still have a second story if you want it for your guests, but you yourself as the senior would be able to live on that one floor if something prevented you from being able to do stairs.

That is a big deal. Inventory is still scarce. And people aren't sure if they want to move. If you live in Highlands Ranch, most people want to stay there unless they're saying, "Well, my grandkids are in California or my grandkids are in Chicago." And then they're looking at maybe an out-of-state move. In that case, I have a really good network of other agents who also specialize in seniors and who would know about the inventory for their specific needs and wants in that city. So once that decision is made, then the process of finding that product is easier. Most of us don't want to let go of what we have until we find what we want. "I'll just stay here if I can't find it."

Kevin: What's the best advice you've ever received?

Pamela: Pray like it's all up to God, and work like it's all up to you.

Kevin: That's great. What would you like to share that I haven't asked you?

Pamela: I should just repeat that in my experience, serving this demographic takes more time and patience. So, for anybody searching for an agent, I think you need to want to deal with somebody who isn't desperate to have your house be their next mortgage payment. Because it isn't that way. It isn't for most of my senior clients. The couple that needed to move to California was like, "It's happening right now." She was not coming back until the house was sold. I got it on the market within two weeks. That is not normal, in my experience. Usually it's conversations along the lines of, "We're thinking about it; okay, we're thinking more about it. What pieces can we do now, so that we are ready if we find what we want and decide to move?" Because then they want to move, and we don't want to have to start from scratch. We don't want to say, "Well, you should have been purging and de-cluttering and that kind of stuff along the way, because it just makes it easier when you finally decide." It helps if they decide early that Grandma's armoire is not going to fit in whatever smaller home they buy. So, as much as we like it, and want to honor the memories, we have to find some ways to honor the memories without taking it with us. I've had people take photographs of hand-made things that were done by their great- great-grandfather in Germany. We take photographs of it, write down a history of it, and find a way to honor it, and that doesn't mean it has to go with them.

Kevin: Where can our audience go to learn more about you?

Pamela: Go to my website, www.denverhomenavigators.com. You can give me a call and we can have a discussion or quick coffee. You can call me at 303-506-0106. That's my cell phone. Those are the best ways to reach me.

Kevin: Awesome. Thank you so much, Pamela.

Pamela: Thank you for your time.

CHAPTER 4

Martha Hartney

Martha Hartney is the principal attorney at Hartney Law, which specializes in estate, business, and family law.

The firm's mission to educate and empower families has touched hundreds of parents. Hartney Law was named Best of the West by YellowScene Magazine the second year it was open, and has won the award six years running.

Martha has also served in the Boulder County District Attorney's Office, Larimer County Domestic Courts, and the Rocky Mountain Children's Law Center. She has served as a pro bono guardian ad litem representing abused and delinquent children, and was also certified as a Child & Family Investigator through the Colorado Bar Association. Martha has also supported new mothers as a La Leche League Leader and has been an advocate of attachment parenting and natural parenting.

Kevin: Martha Hartney is an estate-planning attorney in Boulder. Tell me about your practice.

Martha: I am an estate planner and my primary audience is families with children still at home and their parents. Even though our marketing focuses on families who are still entering their peak earning years, about 25 percent of our clientele are people over 60. We work with seniors as well. At our firm, we help make sure parents' affairs are in order so their children can continue with their lives in a good way. When death arrives or disability occurs, their families are taken care of in a way that they can feel good about, and that they've left something behind that's meaningful.

Part of the value we bring to our clients is our philosophy and beliefs in the importance of estate planning and the opportunity it offers. Many lawyers see estate planning as a set of documents you put in place for worst-case scenario. We believe that estate planning is much more than that. An estate plan is a vision for the future—a set of intentions for our children and their children. It's kind of like setting the bow of a ship for our family's future, with the intention that they reach their destination safely and as smoothly as possible, even if we're not at the helm of that ship. It also sets an example for our families as to how to meet our death carefully, mindfully, and courageously. After all, our children will one day die, as well, and how we die will provide a living legacy for how they, too, should live and die.

When you see estate planning in this way, we can work with financial wealth as the fuel for our family's future, instead of as the end goal itself. In our practice, we ask our clients to get in *right relationship* with money—not as an end in itself, but as a means to a life we can be proud of and that fulfills our mission on earth. Money is not our true legacy. The way we live our lives and how we meet our death are our only real legacy.

Kevin: You'd mentioned that if you don't have a plan, the government has one for you, and it's not in your best interest.

Martha: Yes, that's true. The judicial system had to develop a way to handle the financial realities of death, because so few people plan. It becomes the courts' problem, and so we have the court proceeding known as *probate*. Probate is a judicial proceeding like any other civil proceeding. But one thing people absolutely must know is that probate exists to pay your creditors first and foremost, not to care for your family. Probate must satisfy your debts before your family receives what remains. People are often shocked to find out that merely having a will doesn't avoid this. In fact, just doing a will necessitates probate. A will is the document we refer to only to determine who you want to receive what you have left, if anything.

Kevin: Have you ever come across a client who didn't have a plan in place and needed your help, but was too late?

Martha: Oh, yes. Remarkably, this happens all the time. If a person has passed the point where they had the mental capacity to know what they're doing, they cannot sign a will, a trust or any other legal document. They may not even be able to hire a lawyer. When someone undergoes mental incapacity and has not planned properly, they and their families are frequently going to be involved in a court proceeding called a *conservatorship* or a *guardianship*. When that happens, a judge ostensibly becomes the head-of-household and decision-maker for the family. Most people really don't want that, but do precious little to prevent it.

Additionally, if we get sick, we slam the door on a lot of planning options we could have used if we were healthy, for instance, life insurance. If we get a diagnosis of a serious illness or cancer, it's near impossible to qualify for life insurance, or it becomes prohibitively expensive.

When we get diagnosed with something serious, we've missed a critical opportunity to plan and to provide for our loved ones. One alarming statistic is that 70 percent of Americans will spend some time in a nursing home or skilled-nursing facility. Yet, how many of us have any plan, legally and financially, to carry us through that?

Kevin: People think they have all this money and all this equity in their house, but if they get sick and need long-term care, it's gone—nothing for the inheritance, nothing for the kids.

Martha: What is our average monthly cost of care here? $9,000 or more a month for skilled nursing care in Boulder County? It's a lot of money compared to a long-term care policy premium, which is $4,000 to $6,000 a year. Anytime we see somebody over 50, we suggest that they start talking to long-term practitioners and certified financial planners to help address this very real, very large risk.

Kevin: People will say, "I have to go do my will. I have to do my estate plan," but then don't do it. People don't want to think about mortality. How do you flip it to where they actually enjoy it?

Martha: For one thing, we make it enjoyable, even fun. The concepts we discuss in our design process, which is a two-and-a-half-hour meeting, can be made interesting, relevant, and fascinating. Designing a plan with a skilled and likeable practitioner can be an educational opportunity to explore and master legal concepts, sometimes for the very first time. A lot of people find that engaging. Education is empowering and helps people take better control over their lives and their deaths.

There's another piece that we do in our firm that makes estate planning more of a heart-felt endeavor and creates an experience in which people can explore their existential issues with questions such as, "Have I lived my life well? Am I leaving something left undone, unsaid, or unresolved that I must take care of before I can die with a peaceful heart?"

We create an estate plan in a three-pillared process. We have to have all three of these pillars in place to really know that we've done a good job. When you get to the end of it, it feels like a tremendous relief.

The first pillar is particularly for families whose children are still at home—making sure that their children's care and custody is solid, so the children are never taken by police or child protective services into state custody. We call this a "Children's Emergency Response Plan" or CHERP. A CHERP ensures children stay with family members or known caregivers in an emergency and there's never any question as to who has legal authority over our kids if we're unable to be there for them. You can find out more about this piece at www.gocherp.com.

The second pillar is the financial piece and, as you know, that's what people call *estate planning*. This is where we will help families decide whether a will is really the best financial vehicle for them, or if they should have a revocable living trust in place. That's becoming more widely known, widely accepted, and is a more thorough way to plan for the worst, in many situations.

The final piece makes an estate plan make sense and gives it a heart. We call this last part of a plan the "Illumination Interview" in which we interview our clients on camera to help them share the story of their lives, their love for their children, their love story, and the wisdom they've gathered in their lives.

The Illumination Interview is a parent's opportunity to lay out for their children and grandchildren the emotional, psychological, intellectual, and professional wealth that they've learned throughout their life. In these interviews, parents can offer their descendants some sense of heritage and belonging that is essential to their well-being in an uncertain future. We hope to give survivors a sense of where they've come from, which helps them navigate where they're going. Children and grandchildren will be able to look back at their parents and their grandparents, and have a sense of belonging to a tribe, so they know who they are. They know they were wanted, know that they were loved no matter what the circumstances of their lives have become.

Kevin: One of the big things we see as people retire is that the research shows a very high percentage want to stay in their home as long as they can. You mentioned long-term care. When that issue comes up, how do you address that with your senior clients?

Martha: Financially, we leave this to the professionals to determine how to maintain a client's residence as long as they can. Families need a financial advisor to help them prepare for the possibility of long-term incapacity and how to meet that cash flow demand, and to counsel them to get the right insurance—disability, long-term care, whatever is appropriate for them.

I have seen circumstances in which a reverse mortgage is what someone needs. Legally, if they want to stay in their home, the best thing they can do for themselves is to have a revocable living trust and to consider hiring an advanced Medicaid planner. At the very least, elders should consider putting a revocable living trust in place with a clear decision-maker. A successor trustee who can take over their finances if they become disabled to avoid an expensive conservatorship, and to avoid extensive probate proceedings after death.

The costs to go through conservatorship or guardianship are enormous. They sap the resources right away because they're independent people getting paid X amount of money to manage your assets for you. We want to keep it within the family unit, keep the sovereignty in the family. Generally, a family member or a friend trustee's not going to charge as much as a bank conservator or guardian. We'll have some savings there, and we get to keep our affairs private and out of the court's control.

Kevin: How do you counsel people in choosing a trustee?

Martha: There are two kinds of successor trustees: institutional trustees and family or friend trustees. My preference is to keep financial governance and sovereignty within the family unit, if at all possible. When we name a successor trustee—and remember, the root of trustee is *trust*—it means we're trusting them with the financial care of our families. A trustee has to be extremely trustworthy. They need to be skilled—or able to develop skills of financial stewardship, reporting, record keeping—and be good decision makers. They need to be able to make difficult decisions and stand by them.

Selecting a successor trustee is a great act of faith, and a vote of confidence in the person we select. I don't recommend having children serve as trustees for each other. Siblings should not be put in the position of having power over one another, except in the case of a sibling who is disabled and cannot care for their own inherited assets. Sometimes, a family simply does not have a potential trustee available and they have to name an institution as the successor. In that case, we want to make sure there is an overseer called a Trust Protector who can remove and replace an institutional trustee if needed.

Kevin: Is there a technique you use that you wish more of your clients or more people you interact with knew about?

Martha: 60 to 70 percent of Americans have no plan at all. A minuscule number has a trust. The Swiss Army Knife of estate planning is a revocable living trust, because it can help a large percentage of Americans keep their family governance private and within the control of a family member. Without a revocable living trust, we're putting our families smack dab in the middle of court proceedings. People think when they have a will, that's enough. They'll hold up a will and say, "They don't have to go to probate. I'm not subject to a court, because I've got a will." No, the will is the document that we open probate with. We send it in with a letter that says please open probate. The only thing that a will can do is replace the depository features of statutes that tells who our heirs are, and how they're going to inherit. That's all a will does.

I want to help all the families I meet with understand that a will is not enough for the vast majority of us. We really need a revocable living trust, the Swiss Army Knife of planning, to take our assets out of the court's jurisdiction and handle them privately. The way I visualize this is that most of us are walking through life with our assets in our bare hands. I picture our assets as a tray of cupcakes we've worked very hard to acquire and save, because that's what feeds us, what nourishes us into the future. We walk around with our assets exposed like carrying the tray with our hands. If, as we walk through life, we trip and fall, we are disabled or we die, all of our stuff goes flying to the ground where the court has jurisdiction over it.

If we die, we have to take those cupcakes and put them into a probate where our creditors get their first bite before our heirs get theirs. Creditors first, family second. Conservatorship is similar in that we think of it as *living probate*. In both cases, a judge is the head of the family. And we're paying for the privilege of being at the mercy of courts.

The better plan for most people is to not hold our cupcakes in our naked hands. That's the fatal flaw. If we fix the problem right at the point of origin, we can avoid a lot of the problems and expenses we are exposed to in court proceedings. When we use a revocable living trust, it's like putting our cupcakes in a little red wagon and pulling our wagon through life. If we trip and fall, what happens to our stuff? It's tucked nice and neat in our little red wagon. If we're disabled, then we have tied an instruction manual to the handle of that wagon that says, "Hand my wagon to my successor trustee and manage it according to these instructions." By transferring management and responsibility to our successor trustee in a trust, we can avoid court proceedings.

Kevin: Tell me about a recent client you had that was a senior. What did they need and how did you help them?

Martha: One of my clients, a woman—with two adult children, one of which is disabled—passed away recently. She had a multi-million-dollar estate. She had a trust in place for many years, and then it was discovered that one of her children had this continuing disability, and needed a special needs trust. She amended her trust to include this special kind of trust. Her adult child is now able to continue receiving disability and Medicaid, and the trust can still provide resources that can supplement her, and will last a long time.

The other sibling does not have a disability and is able to serve as the trustee for the disabled sibling. In this case, the mother understood the nature of the children's relationship, how well they could get along, and then matched the planning to that relationship precisely.

When lawyers don't really feel into the nature of the next generation and what could happen at the third and fourth generations, we end up with people in conflict with one another. That's how estate planning can be used improperly and set up for an adversarial relationship in the future. Many estate planners don't really design plans to support good relationships between generations. They tend to see estates from the view of taxation and asset protection as the two primary concerns. In our practice though, I'm looking at complex emotional relationships between parents, children, grandparents and anyone else in the picture. We want to set them up for success as best we can, rather than pit people against each other, which happens in a lot of families due to existing dysfunction or just plain sibling rivalry.

Kevin: Describe an ideal client. What's the type of person you're looking for?

Martha: Our clients are interested in their future, interested in doing things well. People who want to take an inexpensive and cursory approach to their estate plan are not a good fit for us. We're thinking all the way through each issue a family presents to us and follow each to its logical conclusion, and we're taking into account the emotional, relational nature of humans.

Kevin: As you meet with people, what do you ask them to do?

Martha: Our process is three to four meetings. It's a commitment to do it right, and we insist our clients participate in the decision-making process. Each meeting is about two hours long, so we're asking them to invest six to ten hours of their time, plus a fair fee as well. It's not insignificant. Our promise to them is that at the end of it, they will feel complete. They will know they're complete. They can walk away from their planning process, put it on the shelf for a while, and know it's there for them when they need it. What do I want from them? Full participation. I want their heart and mind in the game.

Kevin: How do they come across your firm?

Martha: Many people find us on the internet, through Google. I also speak a lot to parenting groups and we receive a lot of referrals because our clients are deeply impacted by the work with us, and they tell others about their experience. Our goal is to give them an unexpectedly enjoyable and enlivening experience that gave them far more than they ever expected. Their ambassadorship for the work we did together is what really drives our work.

Kevin: Do you do workshops or seminars or dinner meeting?

Martha: I speak to existing groups like moms' and dads' groups once a month, so people are always welcome to come to those. We do webinars online as well. A lot of the content that I offer out in the community is freely available on our website at http://hartleylaw.com/ so people can watch short and sweet educational videos from the comfort of home.

Kevin: What's your biggest challenge right now?

Martha: What's hardest for me is knowing parents need to do their children's planning, but just aren't doing what they're supposed to do. Every single parent in America needs a Children's Emergency Response Plan, but precious few actually have one. It blows my mind that parents cannot find their way to making clear decisions about who will raise their children, then to nominating those guardians, both temporary and long-term, in writing. It's very challenging to me.

There are a handful of reasons why people never get around to nominating guardians. One is that they have issues with their family of origin or their partner's. Thinking about who would raise our children if we die brings up any pain we might have about our families. Another is parents don't want to hurt family members' feelings who aren't being asked to be a guardian. Parents often feel like they need to explain themselves to others. But they don't. Parents don't have to explain themselves to anybody. This is their decision alone. Only a parent can make it. Another is that parents fear working with an attorney, partly because they don't know how fees work and are worried about getting a surprise bill for short phone calls. Or they don't think they can understand all the legal mumbo jumbo. At our firm, we make working with us as easy as possible and have conversations that are understandable and fees that are predictable. We're removing as many of these fear barriers as we can, so that more and more people get their planning done the right way the first time.

Kevin: How do you get people to move, to decide to act?

Martha: Really the decision is the client's, but we want to make sure they're committed to doing what they know they need to do. We start with what's important to them, and identify the things that keep them up at night. We solve those and then we go a few steps further than they even realize they need to go. We can see needs and desires they may not even be aware of when they come in the door. When we reveal some of those, and how to meet those needs, most people don't have any trouble taking action.

Kevin: What would you like to share that I haven't asked you already?

Martha: As an estate planner, I have a strong bias, which is that I believe it is our responsibility to keep our family business out of the court system. Our courts need to be free for those people who simply cannot afford to do good planning. Those of us, who can afford to plan, should plan. Some lawyers are critical of trust lawyers like me, namely probate lawyers, who profit more when people don't do their planning. They'll say things like, "You don't need to avoid probate because probate is easy in this state." I cringe when I hear that. Probate is easy for probate lawyers charging $300 an hour. And they are missing the point. Probate is a public judicial proceeding, which places creditors in a superior position to the family. That's just plain wrong.

Kevin: Why does probate take so long?

Martha: Probate takes a minimum of six months because we have a required creditor notice period of four months. In the notice period, we have to give notice to the world that the person has died. Creditors get a four-month window to make claims against the estate. Plus, it takes a few weeks to open, then a few weeks to close. Even the simplest probates take six months. In more complex and valuable estates, more things have to get done, and more contests and conflicts are likely to arise. Avoiding probate, for many people, is just the right thing to do for families and for our overcrowded courts. The only people who vehemently disagree with that are the lawyers who stand to profit most on probate.

Yes, some families should go to probate. I can make this really simple. If a person has more debt than assets to pay those debts, probate is a good option, because if the money runs out before everyone is paid, the court can cut those creditor claims off and those creditors go away empty-handed.

Kevin: Martha, thank you. This information is extremely valuable.

CHAPTER 5

Aaron Eisenach

Aaron Eisenach is a long-term care specialist. As a broker, he assists people as the proprietor of http://www.aaroneisenach.com, and he supports other agents and agencies as a wholesaler with Individual Commercial Brokerage, Inc. As both a broker and a wholesaler, he works with people across the country.

Aaron has been specializing in this field since 1996. He knows first-hand the importance of long-term care, as he saw both his grandfather and father suffer the effects of Alzheimer's disease.

He is certified by the state of Colorado as a provider of mandatory continuing education classes. Agents in Colorado must complete these courses in order to be able to offer LTC insurance products to clients. Aaron is also sought after as one of the most entertaining and informative speakers on long-term care in the nation.

Kevin: So, I'm with Aaron Eisenach. And what is the name of your company?

Aaron: AaronEisenach.com. I specialize in long-term care planning.

Kevin: Awesome, okay. So, tell us where did you grow up?

Aaron: I grew up in Fort Morgan, Colorado.

Kevin: A native. Tell us about your childhood.

Aaron: I grew up on a family farm. I had great upbringing with three brothers and wonderful parents. I enjoyed 4-H and any sport I could join.

Kevin: Awesome. So, what did you grow on your farm?

Aaron: We had a feedlot for beef cattle. We raised corn and alfalfa hay.

Kevin: My mom grew up on a farm in Canada. Every summer, my brother and I helped bring in the harvest. Boy, that's hard work. Physically very hard work.

Aaron: It is. Yeah, it can be very hard.

Kevin: Long days.

Aaron: It's a way of life and I miss it.

Kevin: Yeah?

Aaron: I miss it to the point where my wife and I actually have about 40 acres and the kids are into 4-H and raising pigs and steers.

Kevin: How about that? That's great. So, how did you get involved with long-term care planning?

Aaron: Well, I lost my dad and granddad to Alzheimer's disease. Plus, my other grandfather spent time in a nursing home before passing away, and one of my grandmothers needed care at home due to cancer. So out of four grandparents, three of them needed long-term care. The fourth died of a heart attack. Then, I had to watch my dad go through the painstaking, awful disease of Alzheimer's. During my very first year in insurance in 1996, I decided that long-term care planning is what I can be passionate about.

Kevin: Yeah, there are lots of directions to go with insurance.

Aaron: Absolutely. I have been blessed to find a niche, helping people with long-term care insurance solutions.

Kevin: So, 21 years?

Aaron: Yes.

Kevin: My dad, too, died of Alzheimer's, or dementia. I'm not sure it was Alzheimer's, but there are lots of forms of it, I guess.

Aaron: Right.

Kevin: You're right. It's just very, very sad. Very difficult illness.

Aaron: It's a very terrible disease.

Kevin: What do you wish you had known when you started, that you now know?

Aaron: How things do not stay the same, that there would be constant change over the years as more and more people need care services. That different types of care services would evolve, mainly home care, keeping people out of nursing homes—and the way the insurance products would morph into something that's a lot different than it was in the heyday of selling long-term care insurance, which was early 2000s.

Kevin: Even better, more choices for people.

Aaron: There are many more choices today. The traditional, stand-alone, long-term care insurance products are much more expensive than in the past. I guess if I had to do it over again, I would've been more aggressive saying that it would be a very bad idea to wait to buy coverage. Prices are going to be significantly higher in the future.

Kevin: It's a bargain.

Aaron: You've got to grab it now—trust me—even though some of those policies have had rate increases. The policies we sold 15 and 20 years ago for traditional long-term care insurance are a fraction of the cost of what they are today. So, I guess I just would have been bolder in my proclamations of, "You've got to do this now."

Kevin: I saw statistics and I want to verify it. Something like 70 percent are going to need some form of long-term care and only seven percent have something?

Aaron: Well, the government stat is that if you make it to 65, you have a 70 percent chance of needing care. I don't know what to really do with that number, because for most people, they don't think it's going to happen to them. I know that it also includes a lot of people who need care for a very short amount of time.

Kevin: Care can start at home even?

Aaron: Correct. Advisors are molded into this idea that if the average stay in a nursing home is just two or three years, that's a small risk. That is very narrow in thinking, because most of the care is at home, not in a nursing home. Most people will do everything they can to stay out of the nursing home. One of the best things about the evolution of the long-term care planning marketplace is putting the emphasis on keeping people at home and out of nursing homes. Now, people are more receptive to the idea of going to assisted living than nursing homes, but again, people are so scared of nursing homes—whether that's founded or not—that they refuse to plan because it's so scary.

Kevin: So, for people who may not know, what's the difference between assisted living and a nursing home?

Aaron: A nursing home is licensed as a skilled nursing facility. It provides rehabilitative, skilled care.

Kevin: So, somebody's sick if they're there?

Aaron: Well, not necessarily sick, though many are. They could be there because they're frail and fragile and need someone's help. They may not be disease-ridden, but there are others that have had a major stroke or are in the throes of dementia or Alzheimer's and are there at the end of life. Assisted living facilities might look more like an apartment. You may move in there by yourself or with your spouse or partner and not need any care. You might be there because you want to have friends and excursions, and by the way, I want to age in place. And if assistance with daily activities such as bathing, dressing, or managing medications is needed, the staff is there to help.

Kevin: So, it's kind of almost like resort living as a senior in some ways.

Aaron: Well, there are degrees of that. There are some that are like a resort and there are others that are more like a basic apartment complex.

Kevin: Just a place to live, make friends, and have your meals prepared for you. To live independently.

Aaron: Right, right. Then if you start to need help, you have reminders for medications or someone to make sure that you're up and awake in the morning. If you start to need help because you're forgetting things, the assisted living facility is there to aid you with those things. Whereas, when we think of a nursing home, we think of people that might be bedridden or maybe they're in a wheelchair. Maybe they need what we call a two-person assist to get from their wheelchair into their bed or vice versa. Chances are that an assisted living facility would not keep someone that needed a two-person assist into the bathtub, into the wheelchair or into the bed.

Kevin: Right. They need more help.

Aaron: So, a higher level of care. The reason they call them skilled nursing facilities is because—let's say that you had a hip replacement, knee replacement, or stroke, and you need physical therapy or speech therapy—that's going to be provided in the nursing home.

Kevin: I see. What are the highlights of your position with what you do?

Aaron: I think the best thing about what I do is I get to meet new people and hear their stories, their experiences. I get to look at all the pictures of the grandkids on the refrigerator door. They'll tell me about what happened to their loved ones and why they're interested in long-term care planning. Sometimes those are very emotional and sad stories, but other times they will say, "We're talking because what happened to my family, I don't want to have happen to my family. What we went through taking care of mom or dad, I don't want my kids going through that." It makes me feel good when we can make those goals come true, make them a reality.

Kevin: Absolutely. Very rewarding. So, when you started in 1996, did you start out on your own or did you work for someone else?

Aaron: One of my brothers who already had a successful insurance agency selling property and casualty insurance took me under his wing and said, "I can't handle the life and health insurance side of the business. I'm too busy with the auto, home, and fire to run the quotes and write the applications for life and health. So, would you like to come and do that?" I said, "You bet. I'll give it a shot." It wasn't, "What?" Six months later or so, I was being more and more attracted to long-term care.

Kevin: Interesting. So, we've kind of touched on this a little bit, but what are some things you do to assist seniors to help them stay in their home, to age in place?

Aaron: Well, I help provide that mechanism, that funding source. And that's what long-term care planning products do. They help fund or give cash flow to their long-term care needs. If that is that they need home care for four hours every other day, here's a policy that can help fund that. Then, if we need to increase those hours to eight hours a day, every day, most people can't afford that. If it turns into home care for 24 hours a day, seven days a week, very few people can afford that. Long-term care planning can make some of those things become a reality.

Kevin: So, really, you're transferring the risk away from yourself to the insurance company?

Aaron: Transferring a portion of the risk, yes. Right.

Kevin: So, Aaron, it's interesting to me that Americans have a lot of insurance. We have auto insurance, homeowner's insurance, health insurance. Some have disability insurance, some life insurance. It's transferring the risk away from yourself, away from your assets, and your family. Why do you think, knowing the statistics, that people are averse to or uninterested in long-term care, when we know 70 percent are going to need it, some form of it? Seven percent have it. We know how expensive it is. Why do you think there's this gap?

Aaron: Because it's scary. We don't ever want it to happen, and try convincing ourselves that we don't need it.

Kevin: So, we just don't want to think about it?

Aaron: I've never met with someone who says, "I can't wait to use this policy." Right? So, when I do public speaking I end the presentation with, "If you buy coverage and you never need it, you and your family will be happy that you never needed it. If you buy the coverage and need it, you and your family will be very happy that you bought it. If you don't buy this coverage and you need it someday, you and your family will desperately wish you had purchased it." I think that there's no getting away from those three points. You really can't argue with them. I don't know about the seven percent figure. It's around 10 percent, especially when you consider that there is a good portion of the population that can't afford long-term care insurance.

Kevin: So, what are people's options? I guess they can self-fund, pay for care they need.

Aaron: I like when you say, "self-fund," instead of "self-insure," because people throw out this term, "We're going to self-insure." There's no such thing because you're not an insurance company. If the cost of care for 12 months in a nursing home today is about $120,000 a year and you are coming up with that money, you are self-funding. Insurance always involves leverage, right?

If you give the insurance company $5,000 a year for a super long-term care policy and you need care someday, it might provide you with hundreds of thousands of dollars in benefits. That's leverage. When you're using your own money, there's no leverage at all. In fact, if you're using qualified funds, IRA money, you have to pay taxes on that. Or if you're selling an asset, you might be paying capital gains, right?

Kevin: Right.

Aaron: You might have to come up with more money to pay for care. There's no such thing as self-insuring.

Kevin: So, number one is self-fund. Number two would be what? Medicaid?

Aaron: Yes, self-fund, Medicaid, or some form of long-term care protection.

Kevin: Let's talk about Medicaid for a second, in case people aren't aware what that is.

Aaron: It will provide care for elderly people that have become impoverished according to the Medicaid guidelines.

Some people will say, "Well, I'm entitled to Medicaid. I paid into it." No, that's Medicare, and Medicare does not pay for long-term care. Ending up on Medicaid means something went very wrong. If we've got someone who's now single or divorced or widowed, for that person to qualify for long-term care Medicaid, assets are limited to a home, which can't be worth more than $560,000 in equity in 2017, a car and $2,000. You can have your personal belongings in the house unless you have a Picasso or a Rembrandt or something like that. You can have your wedding ring set and an irrevocable burial plan and life insurance unless there's more than $1,500 in cash value. Everything else basically has to be down to zero. Annuities are gone. The 401(k) is gone. The pieces of property you inherited are gone. The second house, the RV, the cabin, are all gone in order to get Medicaid.

Kevin: Right. I understand there's also a look-back period. Is that right?

Aaron: Right. If someone tries to get rid of assets by gifting or putting assets into an irrevocable trust, there is a five-year look-back period. There are ways that some attorneys manipulate that, to put it mildly. People need to know that this type of planning has two very big drawbacks. First, Medicaid primarily provides funds for care in the very place no one wants to be, in a nursing home. Second, transferring assets and giving up control means a significant cut into lifestyle. And planning to get Medicaid flies in the face of the idea that we want the best care for our loved ones.

Do you have kids?

Kevin: Yes. I have five.

Aaron: Okay. If you had to go to, say, Bangladesh to find the one physician in the world that can cure your son or daughter of the ailment that they have, you would go to Bangladesh or wherever it is, because you'd want the best. Why is it that some people think that towards the end of life, when we are going through a chronic illness, that we don't care anymore about the quality? I want the best nursing home, the best assisted living facility. I want that 24/seven home care. Yet some people think, "Well, I'm old. It's not going to matter." That's crazy.

Kevin: So, in a Medicaid facility, there are no private rooms?

Aaron: Well, there are facilities that are only private pay. And there are facilities that have a high number of Medicaid beds. Then there are nice facilities that have a small number of Medicaid beds. These places are going to have good reputations, but their Medicaid beds are in high demand. So, let's say that mom or dad or a spouse needs care. We've spent down assets to Medicaid-required levels. We go to these three or four facilities that we've heard good things about. We know that most people there are paying privately, but they have maybe a dozen Medicaid beds available. So, we go to them and say, "Can we get one?" They'll respond, "No. We have a two or three-year waiting list."

Kevin: Is that right?

Aaron: Yes. They'll tell you it is because "we're going to save those beds for the people who have been paying here privately. They're first in line. We'll call you in a couple of years or if something changes, unless the family wants to pay for the care for the next couple of years."

Kevin: So, if I'm understanding, they have a certain number of beds allocated for Medicaid, but because the demand is so great, the private paid people supersede the Medicaid people?

Aaron: Yep.

Kevin: Okay. I do public speaking seminars, too, but I guess another option could be their kids take care of them or they go live with their kids. Every time I say that in a seminar, the people groan out loud. I said, "Don't worry. Your kids don't want you to move in either." If that were to happen, I mean, somebody would have to leave their job to care for mom or dad, right?

It's not like you leave them in the morning and say, "I'll see you at 5:00." I mean, you've got to be there, involved and helping them.

Aaron: Right. When my dad needed care, who did it first? Mom. How long did that last? It lasted until she couldn't do it by herself anymore. Then she turned on his long-term care insurance policy for care. That funded the home care agency to come in and help mom keep dad at home. Sometimes people will say, "My daughter, my son," whomever it is, "they've already said, 'We're going to take care of you.'" Great. But does it have to be 24 hours a day, seven days a week? Do you think it would be nice if you had a home care agency come in and take the morning-to-evening shift, from 8:00 to 5:00? Does the child who's planning on doing this have a spouse and kids and a job? Who is going to set aside their life to keep you at home? One thing that happens often times, especially with people with dementia or Alzheimer's, is someone else's life as they know it, comes to an end, because someone is going to have to be there 24/seven.

People think this is all about protecting assets. It's first and foremost about protecting the emotional and physical wellbeing of the caregiver, which is often times the wife.

Kevin: So, now, let's talk about, I guess, option four, long-term care planning. Why get it and what is it? How does it help people? Why should they want to get it? Et cetera.

Aaron: Okay. I think there are five distinct paths today. In the past, it was always about traditional, stand-alone, long-term care insurance products.

We call it traditional, long-term care insurance, because traditionally that's what we recommended and we all offered it. We call it "stand-alone," long-term care insurance, because there's no death benefit or no cash surrender value. I'll come back to those two things in a minute. So, the traditional long-term care insurance policies are very good for the middle class. Pay ongoing premiums. It's a form of health insurance, health insurance that covers chronic illnesses, because Medicare and health insurance do not. So, that market has consolidated and the policies cost a lot more than they used to. It's pay-as-you-go. If you never use it, you lose it. The second path is life insurance. "Well, I don't want life insurance," many will say. Today, modern life insurance contracts say you can use your death benefit if you need care. We call that an accelerated death benefit. For example, if someone has a $200,000 death benefit, their policy might say, "You can use two percent or four percent of that death benefit per month for care." If there's a $200,000 policy with a four percent accelerator, if you will, you have an $8,000 monthly benefit for long-term care. If you don't use it for long-term care or whenever you don't use the death benefit, that goes to your beneficiaries.

Kevin: Once it runs out, it's exhausted. So, basically, two years in that example?

Aaron: In that example, yes, 25 months. That's the second path. It's very attractive to people who bought life insurance policies years ago that have grown cash surrender value. They might want to do an exchange into a policy that allows them to use it for long-term care.

Kevin: A 1035 tax Exchange.

Aaron: A tax-free, 1035 Exchange, exactly. The third path is the combination of the first two paths. We call this hybrid life insurance or asset-based or combination policies. We start with a small layer of life insurance that pays out to beneficiaries if you don't need care. If you do need care, you accelerate that small life insurance first for care. If you run out of that part, the second half of the hybrid is a long-term care insurance rider. This type of policy is often times for upper-middle class or affluent clients. Sometimes they're funded with a single premium like $100,000, which may someday in the future provide $600,000, $800,000 or one million or more for care. The client knows that their premiums are guaranteed. There's a death benefit if they don't use it for care, and if they cancel the policy someday they get their premium back. Very good for people who maybe just got an inheritance or have cash in the bank doing nothing for them.

The fourth path is very much like the third one. Instead of starting with a life insurance policy, the premium goes into a hybrid annuity. Let's say someone has an existing annuity that is just sitting there. They don't need it for income. They might exchange it for a hybrid annuity that says, "If you need care, you use your own money in the annuity portion first." So, if you need care, you use your annuity value first, followed by a rider that provides more money for care. Here's a quick example: put in $100,000, which turns into $300,000 for care. If care is needed, the first $100,00 that comes out of the hybrid annuity is your own money. The next $200,000 is basically long-term care insurance. Some of the neat things about this type of coverage is that a married couple can share one policy, and if the annuity portion isn't used for care, it is paid as a death benefit to the beneficiaries. Plus, these policies are easier to qualify for with your health.

Then the last path is what we call short-term care insurance. These are getting to be more and more commonplace. They're much like traditional long-term care insurance policies, but they cover, in many cases, up to 360 days of care. They can pay even if Medicare is paying, in some cases. When someone says, "We need to have some long-term care insurance," often times the decision is based on their budget and their health.

Kevin: Good.

Aaron: So, that was a long answer.

Kevin: Yes, that's very helpful. Aaron, what do you see as some of the most common mistakes seniors make as they approach or are in retirement?

Aaron: The first thing is thinking that it's too early to buy long-term care coverage.

Kevin: So, what's the optimal age?

Aaron: There isn't an age to point at and say, "That's the age." You have to buy it when you are healthy enough to do so. You have to do it before the house is on fire. You should do it as soon as you can. I bought my first policy at 35 and my second policy at age 40. So, I carry two of them. Sometimes I'll talk to people in their 70s who say, "Well, we don't want to buy this too soon." They should've bought it 20 years ago. So, when people ask me, "What's the right age to buy?" I say, "Whatever age you are right now is the right age, because you never, ever know when your health could change. And the longer you wait, the more it costs."

Kevin: So, it sounds like you do a lot of education with your senior clients.

Aaron: Certainly, certainly. I'll just tell you, Kevin. I don't use the word seniors unless I'm talking about people graduating from high school to college, because we sell lots of coverage to people in their 40s and 50s. I wouldn't call them seniors.

Kevin: What do you like best about your business, Aaron?

Aaron: Constant change, always looking for the next best insurance product, and like I said earlier, meeting new people and addressing and solving their concerns.

Kevin: Is that hybrid with the annuities in long-term care, relatively new?

Aaron: It's not that it's new. There are some of the life long-term care hybrids that have been around now for 30 years. When we could sell traditional standalone long-term care insurance in the past for under $100 a month with unlimited benefits, why would you ever buy a hybrid back then?

Kevin: Right.

Aaron: So, they've been around. There are more companies offering the life long-term care hybrids than the annuity long-term care hybrids. When interest rates finally go back up someday, there will be many more companies that offer these hybrid long-term care annuities. So, they're not new, but with the large price tag for traditional long-term care insurance today, and if people are in their 60s or 70s or maybe even in their early 80s, we're using some of those alternative plans.

Kevin: Tell us about a recent client that you helped, preferably a senior client. What was their situation? What were they hoping to accomplish, and how did you help them?

Aaron: I helped a couple recently. She has been a part-time caregiver for one of her best friend's spouse who is suffering from dementia, most likely Alzheimer's disease. Her friend is taking care of his wife 24/seven. Their group of close friends take turns once a week helping him take care of her. When people need care, we figure it out. So, with this couple, he's 65 and a physician. She's 62. They wanted to do something about long-term care planning after seeing what it is doing emotionally, physically and financially to her friend. She and her husband purchased hybrid life long-term care solutions that provide indemnity benefits. Indemnity benefits say that as long as you can show the insurance company that you're getting at least a dollar's worth of care this month, perhaps from a home care agency, the full monthly benefit is paid to the insured. Then the monthly benefit provided by the policy can be used for just about anything, including care from family and friends.

Kevin: So, a family member could get paid to care for someone? That's huge.

Aaron: Yeah, and those policies are rare. So, another example. I'm working with a couple in another state right now, both age 73. They have been looking at all these different products from a number of people. They found me on my website, watched some of my videos, and contacted me. I showed them some flaws in the coverage that other agents were recommending and why a different insurance company and product would give them more bang-for-the-buck, plus indemnity benefits. People want to stay at home. If the family is going to be involved, they want to know that the benefits can still flow.

Kevin: Absolutely.

Aaron: I really like doing that.

Kevin: That's cool. Who's an ideal client for you?

Aaron: Gosh. I don't know that there is such a thing, because everybody has different goals, different budgets, and different ways to fund their coverage.

Kevin: Somebody who is open-minded. Somebody who wants to learn. Somebody who is healthy.

Aaron: Someone who can come to grips with the fact that this is the biggest risk left in life, because if you think about it, we can manage our portfolio, our investment risk. We can manage inflation risk. We can manage the risk of our home burning down or having a terrible car accident. We have health insurance and Medicare someday for hospitalizations. According to the Alzheimer's Association, if you make it to age 85, you have a 43 percent chance of developing Alzheimer's disease. If you live long enough to become fragile and frail, what's the plan?

That's what we always try to get through to folks. Having a long-term care plan is not necessarily about having long-term care insurance. Everyone needs a long-term care plan. Who do I want to care for me or who do I not want to care of me? Where might I be living at the time? What if my kids get involved, because they don't know if I'm safe and getting good quality, high quality care? Might they get involved? Might they move in with me or move me in with them? What kind of care would I prefer? Who is going to coordinate all of this? Who is going to hire and fire the home care agency? Who is going to make the decision to place the loved one in an assisted living facility or a nursing home or hospice and how are we going to finance it? So, having a long-term care plan encompasses all of those—who, what, where, why, when, how. All the long-term care products do is help you fund the long-term care costs, if it happens.

Kevin: If you fund your plan. With these ideal clients, what's the first step you'd want them to take and how do they find you?

Aaron: The first step is to get educated. They can find me online where I have some educational videos on the various planning solutions. Not only do I work with individuals referred to me by other clients, a lot of my clients are financial advisors. Financial advisors who say, "Long-term care planning has gotten to be so complicated, so sophisticated. All these changes and all these new products, I don't want to make a mistake. I don't want to take the time to learn all of this. Will you partner up with me?"

So, I do a lot of joint casework. When an advisor has two opportunities, let's say in a year, to discuss long-term care insurance with a client, there's no way they're going to be able to do an adequate job. So, often times, my client is the financial advisor who has me meet with their clients and I help their clients. That has been a huge blessing for me.

In Colorado, I teach the state-mandated CE courses. Those CE courses start with 16 hours of initial training, and then every 24 months, another five hours of training. So, I teach that with a business partner. That's allowed us to give out some 8,000 certificates of completion. That's how I know many of the agents in Colorado.

Kevin: Got you. Aaron, what's the biggest challenge you're facing right now?

Aaron: Finding affordable ways to help people who need the coverage the most. By that, I mean if a long-term care event happens, an accident, or an illness, or old age, it's going to wipe them out. There's going to be serious consequences to the family and the retirement portfolio. How do we help people that don't have much to spend on a good policy? How do we still deliver value to them? That's the hardest thing.

Kevin: What's the best advice you've ever received?

Aaron: Trust in Christ as your Savior.

Kevin: Me, too. Amen to that. What would you like to share that I haven't asked you?

Aaron: I think I already did this, but it's not about the risk of needing care, because, again, people are always like, "What's the chance that I'm going to use this policy?" When I'm sitting with someone, the chance of them using the policy is either zero percent or a hundred percent. It doesn't matter if you have a 50-50 chance or an 80-20 chance.

Kevin: Isn't it funny, we don't ask that about homeowner's insurance or auto insurance?

Aaron: Right. The way I like to discuss it, Kevin, is this. If I have a life insurance policy, a term life insurance policy, they say the chances of you collecting a death benefit on a term life policy is around two percent. Does that mean it's not worth having? No. A two percent chance of dying with a term life policy in force is too high. If we had 100 people in a room and we announced that, "Two of you are going to split the Powerball jackpot tonight," everybody would run out the doors and we would all go buy a Powerball ticket.

Kevin: Good example.

Aaron: Two percent of dying with a term life policy in force is too high, given the consequences to others. So, I tell people in my classes or in my public speaking, "I have long-term care insurance, because I love my wife and kids." Just like I have life insurance, because I love my wife and kids.

Kevin: Right.

Aaron: Just like I have disability insurance, because I love my wife and kids.

Kevin: Where can our audience go to learn more about you?

Aaron: Aaroneisenach.com.

Kevin: Thank you very much, Aaron.

Aaron: You are more than welcome.

CHAPTER 6

Shawn Witkowski

Shawn Witkowski is a partner and senior payroll and taxation accountant at Accounting & Tax Resources, Inc. He processes payroll for more than 100 businesses, and prepares tax returns for more than 400 clients. Shawn also works with established companies on mergers and acquisitions, and advises new companies on business structure. He is a Certified Payroll Specialist, and an Enrolled Agent to practice before the I.R.S.

Previously he served as Director of Finance for the Colorado Wellness Group & Medical Massage Center, where he created budgets and forecasts, developed financial strategies, and managed human resources. He began his career in finance as a tax preparer for H&R Block while attending the University of Northern Colorado.

Kevin: I'm with Shawn Witkowski of Accounting & Tax Resources, Inc. Thanks for taking the time, Shawn.

Shawn: Of course, no problem.

Kevin: We always like to start off finding out about you. Where did you grow up?

Shawn: I grew up right here in Littleton, Colorado, not but two and a half miles from my office here. Great place to live, great place to work.

Kevin: What was your childhood like?

Shawn: What can I say? It was great. My parents have been together since 1975. No divorce is usually a great recipe for anyone's childhood. I have a sister who is five years younger than me and we have always been close. I played hockey, football, baseball, tennis, and golf. I played the saxophone and was in a few plays in high school. I tried to participate in everything to see what I liked, loved and, of course, what I didn't like. Childhood years were very good.

Kevin: What did your parents do when you were growing up?

Shawn: My dad is a CPA and we actually work together here at Accounting & Tax Resources. He's been an accountant since 1988, which is when he started this business. He became a CPA in 1994 and hasn't looked back since. My mom has always been in the accounting and consulting business as well. She also works with my Dad and me. It's a family business with six other dedicated employees that add to our solid team.

Kevin: Oh, that's awesome. What made you want to pursue a career in the tax, accounting, and payroll business?

Shawn: Growing up I said, "I'm never going to do what my dad does." Then I went off to college and it was hard to really pin down what I wanted to do for the rest of my life. I was constantly switching my major and my dad finally said, "Why don't you take an H & R Block course and just see if you like it. If you don't, then that's that."

H & R Block courses, in case you didn't know, teach you how to prepare your own income tax returns. I took the H & R Block course and I happened to be really good at it. It was one of those things that just clicked and I started to really enjoy. After I completed the course, H & R Block offered me a job. I worked for H & R Block for two years

	in college while I completed my bachelor's degree. I guess when you grow up being surrounded by tax from my parents, it unconsciously becomes engrained in you and, as a result, comes naturally.
Kevin:	Wow. What do you wish you had known when you started that you now know?
Shawn:	There are many things. You can write a book on just that. The tax laws are very complicated and constantly changing. I learn new things every day, every month, every year. That's the one thing that's pretty exciting about what I do—I'm always learning something new. It's hard to pinpoint any one particular thing I wish I had known in the beginning.
Kevin:	What are some things that you do to help seniors prepare for their retirement years?
Shawn:	We do retirement planning and how it relates to income taxes. We look at your assets and determine the best way to use those throughout your retirement, without creating a large tax burden. We deal with what revolves around tax.

Secondly, and this may be the hardest thing we do, but we make our senior clients realize that death is inevitable. I know this may sound odd and/or depressing, but we do this so that you can effectively plan your estate. Most people don't want to face this fact, so they ignore it. These are the people that, when they pass away, half their estate goes to taxes. There are so many positive things you can do to plan your estate and leave your beneficiaries exactly what you intended to leave them without potentially paying any taxes. |
| Kevin: | You help people sort through all that stuff? |

Shawn: Correct. Now, we're not lawyers; we're not attorneys. We don't write wills. We make sure everything's in the right place, so that someday, when that day comes, it's pretty easy for the beneficiaries to handle, in an already difficult time.

Kevin: Sure. What do you like best about your position and your role here?

Shawn: I like giving people good news. Unfortunately, that's not always what I get to do. Sometimes I have to deliver bad news, but ultimately, I like to educate people. Tax laws are very complicated, and there are a lot of moving parts. No one's tax situation is exactly the same. It's very important that you educate people so they don't make a huge mistake, like liquidate their retirement before retirement age. All of a sudden, they have this huge tax burden, as well as a 10 percent early withdrawal penalty that they weren't expecting. Education is the best thing you can do for people as far as tax planning goes. If I educate and plan well with my clients, usually I can turn, what would have been bad news, into good news.

Kevin: Awesome. One of the things we find with seniors is they want to stay in their home for as long as they can. What are some ways that you help seniors age in place or stay in their homes?

Shawn: I do completely understand that. I had a grandfather that passed away a few years ago and that was exactly it. He wanted to be in his house for the rest of his life. Unfortunately, there was a point where he could no longer take care of himself and we had to put him in a retirement community. He thought that he was going to get better and return home. It was a sad situation, because it simply wasn't true.

For seniors that want to stay in their home, it can be hard if you require care. The costs associated with in-home care are astronomical compared to someone who could move into a retirement community. I completely understand, though. I wouldn't want to leave my home. Your home is where you have possibly lived for decades, and that's where you want to end up. Reverse mortgages are certainly an option when it comes to staying in your home. You can offset, assuming that the house is not paid off, any mortgage that you may have or if the house is paid off, it can certainly help to offset those in-home nursing care expenses.

Kevin: What are the most common mistakes you see seniors make as they approach or are in retirement?

Shawn: Unfortunately, a common problem I see is people who are living beyond their means or have not put enough money away for retirement and have to return to the work force.

There is also the flip side—people who have more money than they need and they forget or do not take their required minimum distribution (RMD) out of their retirement accounts. There is a 50 percent penalty for not properly taking your RMD. That's money you can save. Penalties and interest are always something that you can avoid if you're planning properly.

I would say the biggest problem I see is when retired seniors are not properly allocating their distributions based on what they need for monthly expenses. Here's a scenario: you have been putting money away all of your life into an IRA, pension, 401k or other retirement savings vehicle. Now it's time to retire. You don't want to take all that out in a lump sum. First and foremost, it could push you into a higher tax bracket and you could end up paying more taxes.

Another concern is most people have Social Security benefits. Social Security benefits by themselves are 100 percent non-taxable; however, if you have other sources of income, the higher that income, the more your Social Security benefits become taxable up to a maximum of 85 percent of benefits taxable. You pull money out of a retirement account, maybe too much, more than you really needed and you thought, "I'll just put it in a savings account." But now, because you did that, you're also making your Social Security benefits taxable as well.

Kevin: Wow. The way you solve these problems is just meet with clients, educate them, and make sure they're aware of different land mines, as it were.

Shawn: Yes. Planning, planning, planning. I see the majority of my clients during tax season, as most people in my field do, but one thing I always encourage is to communicate with me all year. If something changes throughout the year, if something comes up and you need more money out of your retirement, you can always talk to me. We can always put a tax plan together, make sure that you're either withholding enough money to be able to offset any tax liability you have at year-end, and then also make sure that you're not taking out more money than you need.

Kevin: What do you like best about your business, Shawn?

Shawn: Well, it's something that over the past 12 years of doing has come pretty naturally to me and it sounds nerdy, but I enjoy the tax law. I don't know why, but I enjoy reading it and I enjoy the ins and outs of it. What I absolutely love most about the profession/business is it gives me a normal schedule and flexibility so that I can be home with my beautiful wife and tuck my two sons in at night.

Kevin: Cool. Is there a product, a technique or a service that you wish more senior clients knew about?

Shawn: Well, I'm sure you would like me to say a reverse mortgage, right?

Kevin: Well, I think you talked about the estate plan. I think very few people have an estate plan. What I tell people is, "We all have a senior partner and the senior partner gets paid first. Beyond that, is custody of your kids, end of life things, that go into estate planning." A lot of people, like you said, don't like to think about that stuff.

Shawn: Yeah. It's just something you never want to have to face, but unfortunately, it's a reality. It's inevitable. I've seen it happen all too often. There was a situation where a man was married and got divorced. Then maybe 10 years later he got remarried. He's happy with his new wife, but he never updated his beneficiary information on his IRAs and 401(k). He passed away and all of his retirement was left to his ex-wife, who is the beneficiary of that retirement, because it was never updated. We all know that's not what the man wanted. If anyone has retirement, I always ask who's the beneficiary? You want to make sure that's up to date constantly.

Kevin: Something they may have overlooked. Innocently overlooked.

Shawn: Exactly. Innocent, like you said. It wasn't really intentional, it was just a matter of forgetting and poor planning.

Kevin: Tell us about a recent senior client that you helped. What was the situation? What were they trying to do? How did you help them?

Shawn: Actually, I just met with some seniors this morning. It was a husband and wife. They had bought a piece of property in 1982 for $14,000. They never lived there, it was just something that they had on the side. Now, with the real estate market the way it is today, it's a good time to sell. They want to sell this property and they're going to list it for $118,000.

Kevin: That's low basis?

Shawn: Very low basis. They paid $14,000 for it. They did some work to it, so we can build up the basis a little, but they still had over $60,000 that would be subject to capital gains once they sell this property. Like I said earlier, the double-edged sword is that they have Social Security benefits and they have a small amount that they pull out of an IRA, so their Social Security benefits are usually non-taxable. However, when they sell this property, it's going to kick 85 percent of those Social Security benefits into being taxed. Not only do they have the capital gains tax, but they also have tax on their Social Security benefits that they've never had before. That was just education. They came to me wondering what their tax liability was going to be on their capital gains, but they didn't ever consider that this would also make their Social Security benefits taxable.

Kevin: So, did you do a 1031 exchange for them?

Shawn: No, not in this situation, because they weren't looking to buy another piece of property. They were just looking to get rid of this one. For a 1031 exchange, you have to buy a like-kind piece of property. They specifically said the money they take from this is going into a savings account for their nursing home some day when they need it. I gave them final figures, prepared a quarterly estimate and they will pay it once they sell the property. Making a quarterly estimate will allow them to not have any underpayment penalties on this tax. Tax is inevitable, but with the right planning, you can avoid penalties and interest.

Kevin: Who's an ideal client for you and your firm?

Shawn: Well, I know this book is about seniors. Seniors are certainly an ideal client, but really, it's much bigger than saying one type of client is best. We are very referral based, so I would say a big family that really trusts each other would be our ideal client.

Here's an example: a married couple in their mid-50s comes to see us to get their taxes prepared. The wife has prepared their taxes for years, but with all the changing laws over the past several years, she wants to make sure they are being done right. They were contributing to a health savings account for the past two years and were not deducting it. I educate them on this tax deduction and we go back and amend the last two years of returns to get them more money back. In their eyes right now, I am their hero.

They have a son in college and they think, "I don't even know if he has been filing his taxes the last couple of years." They bring me his returns to file. They also have a daughter who just bought her first house with her husband. They say to their daughter, "Go see Shawn. He got us all this money back!" There is another solid client right there.

Then, the father sends his parents who are in their early 80s. We do planning and make sure that they have enough money to cover all their medical expenses. Additionally, they have a large IRA account that they must take the required minimum distributions on. We make sure this is being calculated properly.

Lastly, this large IRA is going to be willed to their children and grandchildren. I am able to do tax and estate planning for both the parents in their 80s, when they pass away someday, as well as the children and grand-children who are the beneficiaries of the IRA.

For the majority of our clients, we do taxes for everyone in their family. This is really beneficial to the whole family when you know everybody's individual tax situation.

Kevin: What would be the first step you'd want these ideal clients to take? Do they fill out something online? Do they just come in with all their stuff? How does your process work?

Shawn: Typically, we have a little phone conversation and then we always want to see all the documentation for preparing a tax return. In addition to that, a copy of the previous years' tax returns, so we have a good feel for your previous tax situation(s). The first step would be to contact us.

Kevin: Okay. What's the biggest challenge you're facing right now?

Shawn: The speculation of everything that is involved with the tax law. There are always changes with a new presidential administration. It doesn't matter if the president is a democrat or a republican, there are always changes. Usually in the beginning it's speculation. It's always hard when a client comes to me and asks, for example, "Well, what's going to change with healthcare next year?" My clients never want to hear this answer but I say, "Your guess is as good as mine." I really don't like to speculate, because it's just not real yet. We just don't have an answer.

A few years back, there was speculation that the limit for a Section 179 deduction was going to be significantly decreased. We had many clients that we tax planned with, that would be affected by this change, but it was all speculation. We didn't know that it didn't pass until the final week in December. It is very hard to tax plan when something like this may have been pushed through, but it's not real until it's in the tax codes.

Kevin: Got it. What's the best advice you've ever received?

Shawn: Treat everyone the way you would like to be treated.

Kevin: That's good.

Shawn: That's always a good one. It puts things in perspective. Everyone has their own problems and demons. And you never really know what's going on in someone else's life, so it's always best to treat someone the way you want to be treated and life should be good.

Kevin: That's good. What would you like to share that we haven't already asked you?

Shawn: Well, I already touched on this a little bit, but not everyone's tax situation is the same. We have clients come in all the time and say, "The guy I work with got a $10,000 refund. Why do I owe $6,000?" I hear that all too often. The bottom line is that everybody's tax situation is different. It could have just been the difference between how you filled out your W-4 when you were hired vs. the person you work with filling it out a different way. Your co-worker's paycheck may have been a lot smaller because they had a lot more going to taxes and that's why they're getting a big refund.

You may think you have a very similar tax situation to one of your friends, and a reverse mortgage, for example, may make a lot of sense for you, but maybe not for your friend. Tax situations are not alike and, additionally, everybody's goals are different.

We have clients all over the spectrum. Some people want to save, save, save, and leave a lot of money to their beneficiaries. Some people want to have a grand finale in

	their life and go through their retirement money more liberally than others. Some people love getting huge refunds, while others hate the idea of giving the government an interest-free loan all year. Everybody's goals are different. We're always here to help.
Kevin:	Where could our audience go to learn more about you and your firm?
Shawn:	Our website is www.ATRItax.com. ATRI stands for Accounting & Tax Resources, Inc. Also, you can always call us, 303-973-0243. We're here year-round and also offer payroll, bookkeeping and business-tax planning services as well.
	We don't have limited hours in the off-season. Monday through Friday we're here.
Kevin:	Thank you very much.
Shawn:	Thank you, Kevin, for this opportunity.

CHAPTER 7

Ken Perrin

Ken Perrin is the senior partner at Financial Foundation Group, which he founded in 2002. His areas of focus include retirement planning, Social Security strategies, health care costs in retirement, 401(k) and investment account management, traditional and Roth IRAs, life insurance and legacy planning.

Ken offers a "high touch" service and consultative approach, with a heavy emphasis on communication for his clients' retirement, life insurance, and tax-managed investing needs.

He holds numerous financial designations, including AIF®, meaning he is an Accredited Investment Fiduciary. Ken says that credential demonstrates his completion of rigorous training and examination requirements, as well as his commitment to professional and ethical conduct.

Kevin: I'm with Ken Perrin from Financial Foundation Group/FFG. He offers securities through Parkland Securities, LLC, member FINRA/SIPC. FFG, however, is independent of Parkland Securities. Ken, let's start by learning a little about you. Where did you come from? How did you get here?

Ken: I was born in Columbus, Ohio, and grew up on the outskirts of Marion, Ohio. We had 17 acres of land, lots of grass to mow, a one-acre garden to take care of, a pond, a river, and lots of trees to cut down and then chop and stack the wood for our wood-burning stove that heated our entire house. It was a great childhood with lots of chores and tasks to do, but that's good. It taught me a lot about hard work. I'm the youngest of three boys. My oldest brother is 10 years older than me, and my middle brother is four years older than me. My mom was a schoolteacher; most of the time teaching second grade, and my dad is a CPA.

Kevin: Awesome. What made you want to pursue a career in the financial planning business?

Ken: Well, honestly, I had never thought much about it coming out of college. I kind of just stumbled on it. But once I learned more about it, I realized that it really put everything together as far as things that I like to do. I've always been very good with math and numbers, but at the same time, I'm very social and outgoing, and always knew I wanted to help people.

Doing what I do now, obviously, I have to be a good financial advisor and planner. I take great care to help my clients with a comprehensive financial plan and with ongoing asset management. At the end of the day though, if you can't communicate all of that well to your clients, and if your clients don't understand what you're doing, they might not have any idea of the great work that you do for them. I really think working with people, developing the relationships, and communicating with people is extremely important. Again, the reason I like financial planning so much is it lets me do both the planning and number crunching for my clients, along with utilizing my people and communication skills in developing the relationships with my clients.

Kevin: That's great. So, Ken, what do you wish you had known when you started, that you now know?

Ken: I wish I had realized at the time how many people really do need the services that I provide. Getting into the business, obviously, you're nervous, you're scared, and you don't have a ton of experience. That slowed my start a little bit. I didn't realize that with the knowledge I had, based on my studying, training and all the different tests I had to take, that even with my limited experience I still had acquired a great deal of knowledge and I could help so many people. I was a little too nervous and scared getting out there and getting started to have the confidence to know that what I did was very, very beneficial to people and there were so many people that needed my help.

Kevin: Absolutely. What are the highlights of your position?

Ken: At this point in my career, my highlights kind of vary from being able to help so many people retire and live their dreams, to owning FFG with my partner, and founding the company 15 years ago. Financial Foundation Group just had its 15-year anniversary, which is something we are all very proud of.

Kevin: Congratulations.

Ken: Thank you. My partner Melissa, and I have worked together for 12 years, and Belinda and Mandy have worked with us for about 10 years each. That is something you don't find in this business very often. We all have very similar mindsets as far as making sure our clients are taken care of, first and foremost. We're constantly working on and developing the company to make it better, to make sure we're taking care of our clients as best as possible, and also making sure we're communicating with our clients as much as we can through a very open, working relationship. Again, working with the same great people for this long has been fantastic. All that being said, I don't think anything really beats the feeling of working with a client for numerous years and helping them reach their retirement goals, confident that they've made a good, well thought-out decision. I love seeing that huge sigh of relief and level of confidence a client has in this process, because we've done such a good job in planning and preparing up to that point.

Kevin: It's very rewarding. The focus of this book is seniors and their children. One of the big things that seniors want, is to live at home as long as they can. They want to age in place. What are some of the ways you help seniors do that?

Ken: Well, first of all, we obviously have to make sure we've done our projections. They've accumulated enough assets, we've got a distribution and retirement income plan in place that's going to meet their expenses, but also plan for the lifestyle that they really want to live in retirement. It's all about planning. It's all about preparation. And it's all about taking into consideration their values and goals. What's most important to my clients? Absolutely people want to stay in their home and we need to know things like whether their mortgage is going to be paid off, what standard of living they're going to have, what their travel agenda is going to be, have they projected for health care and long-term care costs, etc. We have to look at all their expenses, not just in today's dollars, but we've got to project those expenses out throughout their retirement as well.

Kevin: It's really a lot more than just money, isn't it? You're part counselor, part other things.

Ken: I wear many hats and counselor is certainly one of them. Yes. Like I was mentioning earlier, absolutely, I've got to be good at my job. I've got to be an excellent financial planner, but that's a minimum standard. I've got to be a great communicator, too.

Kevin: So, what are some of the most common mistakes you see seniors make as they approach or are in retirement?

Ken: There are a lot of financial plans that fail even though clients thought they were well-planned. They forgot to consider, for example, a long-term care issue. Or they forgot to consider something else to do with healthcare. Or they took Social Security too early, or didn't take taxes into consideration like they needed to, etc. Financial advising, obviously, includes investment management and retirement income and distribution planning, but it is really so much more than that.

We work with clients on their Social Security planning. We help them understand what they should plan for from a healthcare-cost perspective in retirement. We absolutely look at long-term care issues that they may face and we make sure that we've discussed and planned for any area that can help our clients. What I say to a lot of my clients is, "At the end of the day, I want your plan to be well thought out and that includes considering unforeseen events that could derail the plan that we've worked decades to put together."

Another very common mistake that people make is not projecting the amount of income that they're going to need, for how many years, and in more than what today's dollars show. What I mean by that is clients say, and I'll just pick a number, "I want to have $6,000 per month in income when I retire." They're retiring at 60 or 65. But, they forgot to plan for longevity. If you have a married couple at 65, odds are at least one of them is going to live into their 90s, so that's 25-plus years of distributing income from their retirement plans. Also, a lot of clients will think that $6,000 per month, which is $72,000 per year, should be fine for them—even times 25 years. But they forget $6,000 in 15, 20 or 25 years is not going to be worth nearly as much as $6,000 today. They will need a lot more than $6,000 to buy the same amount of stuff later. They don't take into consideration inflation, the costs of goods and services going up, etc. That's definitely a big mistake.

Another big mistake for many people is that they don't realize that if they immediately enter a bear market when they retire, their money can run out much, much quicker than they ever anticipated. They plan for an average rate of return, however the market is never going to get them exactly X percent every single year. The stock market is obviously variable. Bull markets and bear markets are normal and we're going to have both. What people don't realize is that if they retire and the stock market goes negative for a couple years right as they retire, they can run out of money decades before they thought they could.

Kevin: What are some of the ways you help seniors solve these problems?

Ken: Well, first of all, seniors need to know that if they put their financial plan together properly, they don't need to keep swinging for the fences with their investment returns. I always help my clients create a portfolio suitable to their risk tolerance, time frame, and current objectives, all of which may be very different for my senior clients than they were in the past. We need to attempt to make sure the money they need comes in, not just today and tomorrow, but indefinitely, and take into consideration potential market volatility, their life expectancies, potential healthcare costs and concerns, etc. We can provide this planning and risk management through various methods and techniques. It really just depends on what's most appropriate for each individual client.

Kevin: You try to customize a plan.

Ken: Certainly.

Kevin: What do you like best about your business, Ken? When you come in every day, what do you look forward to? What do you enjoy most?

Ken: It's a combination of things. Like I mentioned earlier, I've always been good with numbers and I've always been good with forecasting and putting together realistic plans. They may be complicated plans, but I'm good at simplifying them so my clients can understand them. And I love people, talking to people and developing relationships with people. I love seeing people feel relieved knowing they're in good hands. So, I guess what I like best is I get to do both. I get to put on my analytical hat. I get to crunch numbers, and I get to dig deep and get into the weeds and put together a plan that takes a lot of work and a lot of thought. But then, I also like to be able to simplify all that work, and make it make sense to a client, and make them comfortable and confident in what they have. They know they can always come to me with whatever kind of question, comment, or concern that they might have, because we do have such a strong relationship that we've built over time.

Kevin: That's great. Is there a product, technique, or service you offer you wish more of your senior clients knew about?

Ken: Yes. I wish more people knew they could use their life insurance policy to double as a long-term care policy as well. I've seen many well-thought-out and even well-funded retirement plans kind of get dismantled because of long-term care issues and costs. That is certainly a case for long-term care coverage. And I believe in long term-care coverage 100 percent.

But at the same time, the thing I don't like about most long-term care policies is that you're basically flipping a coin. If that coin lands on tails, they may have spent decades funding a long-term care policy and then get nothing in return because they never ended up needing long-term care. I wish my senior clients, in fact, all clients, knew that you can use life insurance to provide long-term care benefits the same way you could qualify for long-term benefits in a long-term care policy.

Kevin: So, it's like a hybrid?

Ken: Yes. It's like a hybrid and, again, it's not a "use-it-or-lose-it" type of plan like most long-term care policies, where it's possible to spend decades funding one, and if long term care benefits are never needed, all of that money is forfeited. With a life insurance policy with LTC benefits as well, it can be used for long-term care or the death benefit can be used to pass on tax-free proceeds to beneficiaries. At a minimum, a tax-free legacy is created for the insured beneficiaries.

Kevin: Great information. Ken, can you give me a specific example of how you help your senior clients?

Ken: Many times, I work with clients that are hoping to retire soon. If it's a married couple, one may feel pretty comfortable, while the other may have some serious feelings of uncertainty and anxiety with this big of a decision. Sometimes both the husband and wife have questions and feelings such as, "Oh, my gosh, it looks good on paper, but do we have all our T's crossed? Do we have all our I's dotted? Are we thinking about everything we need to think about as we take this next step into retirement? Are there things we're not thinking about?"

This type of situation is very, very normal. If clients are retiring early this could lead to more stress thinking about how inflation is going to mean they're going to need a lot more money down the road. Things look good on paper in today's dollars, but there are just so many questions and possibly nagging feelings that they are not 100 percent confident in, which can really eat someone up inside. Often clients wonder if they really do have enough money.

In my planning I will look at all of my clients' different classes of assets and talk to them about their specific goals and objectives. I take into consideration inflation, longevity, taxes, and projected returns. I need to know what they want to protect against, from uncertain markets and uncertain health care costs. Most of the time there are things people do not think about which could potentially dismantle their plan. After careful consideration and discussion regarding all these areas, ultimately, I hope to provide clarity and have my clients in a situation where they breathe easy and sleep well at night.

Kevin: That's so important. Ken, tell us about an ideal client for you.

Ken: First and foremost, clients need to know what I do, but they also need to know what I don't do. I'm not your get-rich-quick type of advisor. I stick to the long-term fundamentals that work over time with investing. My ideal clients know what they don't know, and they understand that they need some professional advice from somebody who's been doing it for 20 years, been through some of the most volatile stock markets in recent history, and knows how to manage risk for his clients in those types of markets. Clients closer to retirement or in retirement may not have time to make up for big losses any longer.

Clients who know what they don't know, clients who realize it's time to take their financial plan, or maybe lack thereof, more seriously, and understand that they need a professional coach, or advisor, to guide them through the complexities of their financial world. That's my ideal client.

Kevin: So, your financial planning would look like minimizing taxes, passing on more money to their heirs, giving money to charity, those kinds of things?

Ken: Yes, absolutely. Taxes are huge. Look at the taxes that my clients are paying on the money they're withdrawing from their retirement vehicles. A strategy I like to utilize is to build up two different buckets of money for my clients. Traditional 401(k) or IRA money that is going to be taxable, and hopefully over time we've also built up some tax-free buckets of money through Roth IRAs, Roth 401(k)'s, and other avenues to supplement the taxable income. That way we can only take what we want to take out of the taxable investments to keep them in, for example, the 15 percent tax bracket, and then just take the extra income they need out of the tax-free buckets.

This could potentially keep them in the lowest feasibly possible tax bracket. That's very important.

To your point as well, Kevin, ultimately my job also has to do with passing money on to their heirs as efficiently as possible, which obviously includes tax efficiency. We don't want Uncle Sam getting a third or more of the assets. He wants it, but hopefully we'll minimize that cut.

Kevin: How do your ideal clients find you?

Ken: Mostly through referrals. Again, I'm huge on communication with my clients. I think no matter what type of relationship you're in, whether personal or business or anything else, in order to have a good relationship, communication is one of the cornerstones. We constantly strive to communicate as best as we can with our clients. All my clients get a weekly email from me, and whether they read it every week or never read it, what's most important is that my clients hear from me and see me every single week. At least they see my name every week through that email. If there's anything that has bothered them, from some noise they heard on the news or whatever, clients can just reply back to that email, or my direct line is on that email as well, and just let me know how I can help.

We also do a handful of client events per year. About half of them are educational events. Later this year we're doing one specifically called, *The State of Your Estate*, to make sure clients are thinking about everything they need to when it comes to estate planning.

We've done tax planning, Social Security strategies, and market update workshops. We've done workshops on women in investing, because the majority of the time the women will be inheriting the assets, and they need to make sure that things are in line and set up properly so Uncle Sam doesn't beat them up too badly, and so they know how to take care of those assets when they receive them.

Again, half our events are educational. The other half are just client appreciation and fun type of events. We've done holiday gift wrapping and open house parties. Most years we do a fun spring cleaning day with our clients where we grill hot dogs, burgers and brats along with sides and drinks and we also have kids' games so our clients can bring their family, grandkids, etc. We do this right after tax time so people can bring in any documents they need to get rid of through a shred truck we rent. We also partner with the Denver Rescue Mission for this event, so people can donate clothes, shoes, furniture, etc., to the Rescue Mission. We also include free electronic recycling and wiping out any hard drives people need to wipe out. It's really a great event each year.

All of these events are designed to really focus on the relationship that we have with our clients. And we always encourage our clients to bring guests to any of these events, so we meet a lot of new people that way. We also meet a lot of new people just through standard referrals that we are given, because of the great work we do for our clients and the relationships we've developed. Our clients know and understand that we're good at our jobs, but they also understand that they can trust us.

Kevin: That's awesome. Ken, what would you say is the biggest challenge you're facing right now?

Ken: Uncertainty in the stock market. The fundamentals look good, and long term, the stock market should do well. But like I mentioned earlier, there are bull markets and there are bear markets, both of which are normal. Bear markets, by definition, mean the markets are down 20 percent or more. Short-term issues that cause recessions need to be corrected and ultimately get corrected. Many times, what causes the most severe dips in the market is simply investor panic. And that is the scariest uncertainty for the markets, in my opinion, since no one can predict how people will react with their emotions.

Those emotional reactions certainly work the other way around as well. The current bull market has been going for over eight years. It's the second longest bull market that we've had since World War II, and it's not normal for the bull market to run this long. It's possible that everyone is simply investing in the market right now because it's been so good for so long, and people are starting to forget that another bear market will happen at some point. I think these incredible runs in the market lead to clients having unrealistic expectations.

Nobody has the crystal ball. Nobody can tell you exactly when a bear market's going to hit, why it's going to hit, or how severe it's going to be. Nobody knows for certain where the bottom is and when you should get your money in there to buy low and nobody knows exactly where the top is and when you should start to sell. Again, that's the most challenging part. You need to set realistic expectations with your clients and make sure they understand the cyclical nature of markets in general, and teach them what they need to do to protect their money from market volatility—especially if they're in retirement or coming up to retirement. You can certainly guide your clients through some tumultuous short-term issues.

Kevin: What would be the best advice you've ever received?

Ken: I would say the best advice I ever received was really more through example than through specific language. It was through my parents. Again, growing up somewhat humbly in Ohio, my parents always lived within their means. They never spent more than they had, and they were always frugal. They really valued a dollar and what it was worth. They valued the work that it took to create that dollar, or now, in my case with my clients, what it took to save your dollars and then protect those dollars. It's really given me an overall appreciation of money and made me want to make sure that my clients' money, and my family's money, is taken care of and that it's looked after well. Again, I appreciate the value of a dollar, and I appreciate the sacrifice that clients made over decades of time in order to accumulate the assets they have. I just want to make sure that money is well cared for.

Kevin: What would you like to share that I haven't asked you?

Ken: Obviously, I could talk a lot about my practice, and how great it is and how great the people are that work here. And all of that is true. I'm very proud of what we have built over 15 years, and I'm especially excited right now, because we're having our 15-year anniversary as we speak. And that certainly adds to another level of enthusiasm.

That all said, what I'd really like to share is bigger than that. It's more about wanting clients not to be scared to talk to somebody. I think there are so many people that don't want to talk to an advisor like myself simply because they're scared of what we might say to them. They may be scared of us looking down on them for not doing a good enough job, for not looking after their assets appropriately over time, or for not even understanding what they have or what to expect from not having any plan put together whatsoever.

Clients should not be scared or intimidated. This isn't what they do. They've worked their entire lives in a completely different business and industry. On top of that, even after they get home and they're tired from a hard day's work, they've got families to look after and to take care of. My business is, to most people, not their native language. I never, ever want my clients to feel like they haven't put enough thought into their financial planning when they come in to meet with me for the first time.

I understand their lives are different, and they don't spend 40 to 50 hours a week in this industry like I do. When my clients come in, I'm just excited they are there and are looking for the help that they need in this complicated field. I would never expect someone to know everything they need to know about my industry without serving in this field. Don't be scared to talk to somebody about how you could make your plans better and take care of your assets more appropriately.

Kevin: Where can our audience go to learn more about you?

Ken: A few different places. Our website talks a lot about our practice and the specific clientele that we look to work with, such as Baby Boomers. My website is http://www.financialfoundationgroup.com. That will tell you about our practice, each of our team members, our backgrounds, both professional and personal, how we grew up and were raised, how and why we got into this business, etc.

We're also on social media. You can follow us on Twitter or you can look at each of our LinkedIn pages. But I would say our website is certainly the place to start. From there, you can always reach out to us, ask any question that you might have, or just let us know if you want to get on our weekly email list so you can hear from us each week. You can find out about the free educational workshops that we offer throughout the year, and you can come to the free, fun and relationship building events that we do throughout the year as well. Our office is located at:

10 Inverness Drive, E #229
Centennial, CO 80112

Kevin: Thank you so much, Ken.

CHAPTER 8

Carol Gosselin

Carol Gosselin is an independent Medicare insurance broker, and owner of Gosselin Senior Health Advisors, which she founded in 2009. She is an expert in Medicare plans, including Medicare Supplement, Medicare Part D, and Medicare Advantage. She represents all major Medicare health insurance plans in the Denver Metro area.

Carol found her calling as a Medicare broker after 35 years in corporate America, where she held outside sales positions for copier and printer companies.

Carol loves meeting people in their homes, work, coffee shops and libraries to educate older Americans about their Medicare coverage, and to assist them in choosing the right Medicare health plan for them.

Kevin: I'm with Carol Gosselin of Gosselin Senior Health Advisors. Thanks for being willing to be interviewed for our book, Carol.

Carol: Thank you. It's my pleasure.

Kevin: We always like to start off finding out where you came from. So, where did you grow up?

Carol: I grew up in the Northeast with most of my employment in the Southeast in the Florida and Georgia area.

I've been out in Colorado since the early '90s and happily married for 30-plus years. My husband and I moved to Colorado back in 1990 to be with children and now grandkids!

Kevin: That's awesome. We're coming up on 29 later this year, so we're a little behind you. What was your childhood like? What did your parents do?

Carol: I'm one of four children, a middle female so I followed my dad in sales. I've been in sales my whole life. My mom stayed at home; she raised four kids. My dad was in sales, outside sales. He did a number of things, including his latest, which was selling large national construction equipment.

He's always been in sales, and that kind of drove me to want to be independent as well. So, I started out selling photocopiers back in the early '80s and dictation equipment. Nobody but those of us 50-plus, knows what the heck I'm talking about. When I say dictation equipment, I mean Dictaphone.

Kevin: I remember.

Carol: Yes, you have to be in your 50s. "Dictaphone? What's dictation equipment?" It still exists, but more in the hospital and higher scale environment where auto voice activation is present.

Kevin: Oh, I see.

Carol: I did that for a little while and got back into copiers, where I was most successful. I had fun, went on Presidents Club trips, where we were recognized for high achievement in sales. Overall, I got to see many places in the world I probably wouldn't have otherwise. I was incredibly blessed.

Kevin: What made you want to spend your time focusing on helping seniors?

Carol: It sort of fell upon me. Being a very spiritual person all my life, I did a lot of talking to God, to help me make change in my life for other people.

Kevin: And He did.

Carol: And He did. I literally stumbled upon it on through an ad I saw on CareerBuilder. I knew I wanted to get into the insurance world and figured that's a great place to retire and I can work as long as I want in that field. You kind of know that in your profession, as realtors do and lots of others, that can be independent well into their retirement years. While I was still working my other job, I studied the insurance business at night and learned the business on the side. I took all the required state and federal tests, and wound up in the property, casualty, and life insurance business for quite a while. I enjoyed it for a short while, but still didn't feel like I was making a difference. I suppose the older you get, you want to feel that warm and fuzzy.

Kevin: Yeah, it wasn't your passion.

Carol: It wasn't. I loved the flexibility, and I love the industry itself and helping folks prepare for lifetime expenses such as life insurance. I was passionate about the life insurance piece, just not so much as the seemingly, lack of loyalty that seemed to occur with helping someone with their automobile insurance coverage.

Kevin: It's true.

Carol: So, I said how else can I really make a difference?

Kevin: Geico makes a living off that, right?

Carol: Yes. I couldn't believe, "Oh golly, you're going to go somewhere else, because you're saving five dollars and I haven't serviced you well enough over the past five years." So, I said, "Well, there's no loyalty here, what can I do to help and really feel like I'm giving back, in a way?"

So, Humana came into my life, and I became an employee of Humana in their senior market division. I really have found, probably my best person, my best profile, and the best of me in the people that I serve. It's that "seasoned citizen," that is very vulnerable and at the same time truly trusting, but often seems to be taken advantage of more so than any other age group. My mother went through that recently. She had a stranger convince her to send him money for his "cause," which of course, has made me even more passionate about protecting seniors and making sure I'm doing the right thing for them. I really feel like I'm giving back to that individual through my time and expertise in the Medicare healthcare environment. Even when I can't help someone after visiting with them in their home, I leave their house knowing I've educated another senior, made a friend and been an advocate for them.

Kevin: Absolutely. That's awesome. What do you wish you had known when you started, that you know now?

Carol: Well, I wish I'd found this industry a lot earlier in my career! But we have no control over timing in our lives. Although, a lot of the new products I sell weren't out then. You know, knowledge is so important. It's something that, in my business, I'm required to learn very, very quickly. The pace of things gets very fast toward the Medicare open enrollment time every year. People often ask me if I'm a nurse, because I get to know medications by name so well. But, now, there's really nothing I'd change. I'm so appreciative.

Kevin: Which is, what? About two months?

Carol: Yeah, about 52 days.

Kevin: Quite a lot. Yeah.

Carol: During that period between mid-October to the first week of December is when seniors get absolutely bombarded with mail from insurance companies. They feel like they have to do something. They pick up the phone and call and invite an agent into their home to help them understand their Medicare choices better. That's where I come in. That's when it gets busy and fun times begin—when I'm with a Medicare beneficiary at their request, and informing them of the many health plan choices for the upcoming calendar year. So, I stay very organized, prep my daily meals, and fill up the crates in my trunk—I almost live in my car for about 50 days. My family doesn't see me very much!

Kevin: How did you come to start your own company?

Carol: I love to network, and wanted my own time to be around the community, without being told I couldn't. I love to be around people, groups and gatherings—getting to know how people help each other, especially those who assist seniors. I joined the South Metro Denver Realtor Association (SMDRA) over 10 years ago, and I was getting a lot of comments such as, "Oh, you only represent Humana." A lot of them wanted to enroll in a different healthcare plan or some of them wanted to know their options. I couldn't offer that to them, because I was captive with just one health plan carrier.

I was recovering from a long illness. I had to get through that and get completely healed. I had to feel like I was in a position where I could be strong enough and stable enough. And my husband and I agreed that this is a time where I can walk away from all I have built with the company and start my own business. That's something I wish I had done 10 years ago, but I grew an enormous amount of experience working for a company with the support and backing of the salary and the benefits and all that in order to know what I needed to prepare for in my own business.

Kevin: Awesome. What would you say are the highlights of what you do?

Carol: I help and enroll seniors in their Medicare health plan choices all year round.

When someone turns 65 and is eligible for Medicare benefits, upon their request, I am invited to speak with them about their choices, and educate them about what Medicare offers.

I enjoy meeting new people, and making a difference in people's lives. The other benefit is making new friends from referrals of my clients. When I walk out of their house they want to give me a hug, because they feel totally at peace. When they say, "She did the right thing, thank you so much," it makes me feel like there's a reward there, and there truly is. I continue to serve seniors all throughout the year with any questions they may have with their health insurance. This business is extremely confusing and hard to manage—mail, understanding claims, etc. Many seniors don't have anyone—family or friends—to help them. I become their trusted agent for years.

Kevin: That's great.

Carol: The rewards are not only financial—this is important of course—but also friendships. When that new client gives your name to someone who is turning 65 and needs help navigating the confusing world of Medicare, that's an enormous reward right there. Getting that phone call is truly the best compliment, right?

Kevin: That's how I work, too, by referral. It's the best way. So, one of the big things we like to do is help seniors stay in their homes as long as they can, to age in place. Is there anything that you do to help make that possible?

Carol: Yes, I reach out to those that assist in home healthcare, medical or non-medical, most often private-pay, and my friends who are senior placement professionals, nurses, therapists, elder law attorneys, financial planning professionals, and more. That's what contributes to that senior staying within their secure environment for years, of course, if that is possible with accessibility. I surround myself with a very large network of resources. I attend a lot of associations and a lot of groups, from senior support groups to senior forums.

Oftentimes, when I talk to them or visit them again to make sure that they're getting the most out of their health plan, they might say to me, "Well, I think I'm going to sell my house. I don't know what to do. Somebody handed me this big old senior blue book here and I'm supposed to find a place to live. I only have this much money to live on." So, I offer them some resources, "Here's somebody I know that can help you. This is a senior placement agency that I trust that has done a good job." Or I help them apply for Medicaid, if eligible, or other federal programs that will help them pay for some of the costs to help save them some money on medications. The best thing I can do is put them in touch with the resources that are the experts, because I'm not the expert when it comes to selling their home.

Kevin: And you're a networker, so that's natural for you.

Carol: Yes. If I can't help them, I'll find someone who will. So, really, it's a matter of all of us making sure we have our resources available for our seniors, from transportation concerns to finding a family attorney.

Kevin: Right, just do what we can to help them.

Carol: There are a lot of resources out there and a lot of seniors don't know about them. It's just overwhelming with all the information.

Kevin: It is. It really is. That's one of the reasons we're doing this book. What are some of the most common mistakes you see seniors make as they approach or are in retirement?

Carol: Seniors living with family members, because they haven't saved enough money, or have been financially over-involved with supporting their children and grandchildren. I was in a client's home yesterday. There is nothing wrong with providing a great family setting for your parents, so they can enjoy their grandchildren. Too often, I see what tends to that financial responsibly putting a strain on the older parents. In some cases, kids will move back into the mom and dad's house. Then the senior is responsible for preparing food, taking care of the kids and giving their Social Security income to the household. And now that senior has three generations in the house and it puts a lot of stress and pressure on the senior, and then their health begins to decline. Financial burdens lead to depression, which leads to other unhealthy living situations. It's very difficult, too, because they want their grandkids around all the time. I see it all the time; they don't get to doctor's appointments, and they don't do proper preventative services, because they don't have time, or they don't have transportation. They had to babysit, or it's summertime and the kids are around all day long and Grandma or Grandpa is there to take care of them. Colorado is an expensive place to live for a senior on a fixed income with only a Social Security check. So, families blend together, which sometimes works great, but in many cases, not for the senior.

Kevin: What do you like best about what you do?

Carol: The joy of running your own business in general and being able to meet and gather with new friends. I have formed wonderful friendships with my clients, and of course get emotionally attached when they pass away. I love the flexibility, being able to just pick up the phone and chat with my client, no matter where I am. Oftentimes, they don't keep track of time—and Friday night at nine isn't often the best time to chat!

I think it's important to be there to service a senior when a bill or a claim comes in and they panic, and don't know who to call. They call me. Insurance is confusing, just the whole process and it makes them feel at ease when they know they can call me to get some answers.

So, it's great to be able to plan my own day and be around people. Again, it's the gather and networking environment that I appreciate so much. If I'm not with the senior, I'm out talking to people who service seniors, so that they can know that I can help them as much as anybody else can in their healthcare.

Kevin: That's awesome. Is there a product, technique, or service you offer that you wish more seniors knew about?

Carol: Turning age 65, and getting their Medicare benefits, but NOT signing up for a Part D prescription drug plan.

I see a lot of seniors missing the importance of having proper insurance coverage, specifically, prescription drug coverage. A lot of seniors are terribly mistaken when they think, "I'll stay as healthy as I can, and if I don't have to take any medications, I don't have to buy a drug plan and spend money on a premium." They are actually incurring a penalty by not buying a drug plan. Additionally, if they are higher income earners, their penalty is even greater.

That's because, Medicare has a right to charge them a penalty, (which is in the form of a tax) for *not* buying a drug plan, even though they say they're so healthy and they're buying drugs that are so very cheap. But, if they don't buy a drug plan, the cost of the penalty goes up every year. And with every annual open enrollment that they don't buy one, it gets higher and higher. I've seen this time and time again where seniors are paying an additional penalty of $20 to $30 to Medicare, because they haven't had drug coverage for 10, 15, or 20 years.

So, I tell everybody I know to tell everybody they know, that even if you are healthy and insist on not taking medications, make sure you buy a drug plan. Some get very angry, because I'm the one that has to bring this up.

Kevin: You're the bearer of bad news.

Carol: Yes, I'm the bearer of bad news on this, for sure.

Kevin: So, tell me about a recent client that you helped. What was their situation? What were they hoping to accomplish? And how did you help them?

Carol: I'm thinking of a client that's been on Medicare for most of her adult life, due to some very chronic illness conditions. She was referred to me by a friend, who thought she needed a lot of hand-holding.

She and I talked for weeks before we met. That really helped me prepare. I like to do a lot of homework, as much as I can, to help prepare that client and help them understand. Because, like many of the people that I work with, she had some forgetfulness issues due to some traumatic brain injuries. I want to do anything to help where she needs some other help or maybe a power of attorney to help speak on her behalf. So, I wanted to make sure I did my appropriate pre-work. I spent probably an hour on the phone with her, trying to fix something that her friend unknowingly messed up.

Lots of comforting, and time.

Turns out, I really made a huge difference in her life by saving her a lot of money on some medical premium. Now she has coverage through her Medicare and a secondary plan.

So much communication is done online, but a great number of seniors don't have computer access. And navigating a computer and systems, isn't easy for a senior. I kind of became that friend for her to lean on. So, she's forever grateful, and I'm happy for that. For me, it's seeing a smile on her face and knowing that I did the right thing. I know in my heart, and God looking over me, that I did the right thing.

Kevin: Yeah, it sounds like you're an extra-miler. You go the extra mile.

Carol: Yes. Well, I think that's very important to do. Seniors are so very appreciative.

Kevin: Who's an ideal client for you Carol?

Carol: Someone who is approaching age 65, who's maybe 64 and a half and who wants to learn more about their Medicare choices.

I help them to compare an employer plan with their Medicare coverage, which oftentimes determines the continuation of part-time or full-time work. And in a lot of cases, it might be a good idea for them to do so.

So many people put Medicare on their radar very early, because they know it's such a confusing topic, which is good preparation. I have sat down with people in many different situations. For example, a teacher who has PERA benefits, someone who has government benefits for Medicare, and others who have individual plans or other employer-sponsored plans. I help them compare the differences and help them make a choice on what's the best choice for them.

Kevin: Wow.

Carol: I'm again, a great resource, and hope to be hired as their agent and friend. Education is important, year after year, in this subject matter.

Kevin: So, these ideal clients, what's the first step you'd want them to take?

Carol: Call me. I'll best direct them as to what to do next, based on their situation. I offer private meetings at NO cost to the consumer. Or, they can attend one of the Medicare workshops or seminars I conduct throughout the year.

Kevin: That's awesome.

Carol: Building awareness.

Kevin: Yeah. What's the biggest challenge you're facing right now?

Carol: I think anybody in their own business could always use more clients. Time management, getting time away with the family—which is what really prompted this challenge!

I could always be busier, really just having enough resources and funds to support all the things that I want to do and all the places I want to be. Isn't it always a financial challenge, marketing yourself? Also, in my case, sometimes compliancy and regulations prevent a lot of creative marketing ideas!

Kevin: What would you say is the best advice you ever received?

Carol: Don't take it personally. I first started selling photocopiers when I was 23. I had a really hardcore female manager who was really, really tough. I was young, not outgoing at the time, and it was my first sales job out of college. On one of my first sales calls to a business, I was accompanied by this manager. I didn't approach the call the way she told me to. I wasn't aggressive enough and she blamed me. I didn't go for the sale and she chewed me out in the parking lot for 20 minutes. You better believe that I didn't let her come to any more sales closings after that!

Learned quickly to just not take it personally. They're saying no because of my offer, not because they don't like me. It took me awhile to get that.

Kevin: Good perspective.

Carol: I had to build the backbone, a little thicker skin, and just keep it up, and not quit.

I was extremely successful by just taking that advice. I never did give her the credit, saying, "You taught me so much." I ran into her probably ten years later. I didn't really think I needed to praise her for chewing me out, but when I look back on that moment, and it was a long time ago, it probably made the biggest difference in my life.

Kevin: You used it to motivate yourself. What would you like to share that I haven't asked you?

Carol: I just love my business, I love what I do. I'm rewarded every day. Be grateful for everything and expect nothing. There we go. Reputation of doing the right thing for the client, can't be bought. It's not the WIFFM business, "What's in it for me?" It's, "What will be the best for the person I'm serving?"

Kevin: I would say that. What's in it for me? Yeah.

Carol: You have to really look at your client and say this is what I believe; it's just how I was raised.

Kevin: That's a good way to live, isn't it?

Carol: To live with morals and ethics that you get to do right with one person so they have the ability to pass it on to another.

Kevin: I live the same way. Where can our audience go to learn more about you?

Carol: Call me by phone or text: 303-250-5605.
Email: carolgosselin@aol.com.
LinkedIn: SMDRA - South Metro Denver Realtor Association – Affiliate Member South Senior Coalition meetings and members

I have a list of financial planners (with their permission to mention) elder law attorneys, home health care aids, senior placement professionals.

I've been working in this business for 10 years; I know a lot of folks, and of course, am out in the community often to nurture relationships.

Kevin: It is more about awareness.

Carol: Just awareness of the products that I represent. So, I prefer they call me and contact me via email, text or phone.

Kevin: Awesome. Thank you so much.

Carol: Thank you.

CHAPTER 9

Anne McMichael

Anne McMichael is a senior counsel at Coombe Curry Rich & Jarvis. She joined the firm in 2015 as an associate, and was promoted to Senior Counsel in February 2017. Prior to that, she practiced at an insurance defense firm.

Anne's practice focuses on a broad array of civil litigation including insurance defense and the representation of small businesses. When not in the courtroom, she assists individuals and couples prepare for the future with estate planning. She is a frequent speaker on that topic at numerous functions throughout the front range.

Anne is a member of the Colorado Bar Association, Denver Bar Association, Colorado Defense Lawyers Association, and serves on the Professional Advancement Committee at the Colorado Women's Bar Association. She is a graduate of Colorado State University and the University of Denver, Sturm College of Law.

Kevin: Continuing on with Anne McMichael. She's an Estate Planning Attorney with Coombe, Curry, Rich & Jarvis in Denver.

So, Anne, do you have any personal experience with how an estate plan has helped your family?

Anne: I do. When I was 18, my dad was diagnosed with ALS, which is a terminal disease. It's an absolutely devastating diagnosis. And it was really important at that point for him to take a hard look at his life and his future and get his plans in order, and that included doing an estate plan. It was incredibly important to have a power of attorney in place, both medical and financial. These documents have actually come in to play a few times throughout his illness. We were incredibly grateful to have them in times of emergency when my dad was too sick to make his own decisions. I know from personal experience how important it is to have this documentation in place before you need it. And that's my aim: to reach out to as many people as possible who have been diagnosed with something or who are in a stage of life where these documents are really important. Estate planning is so important for everyone.

Kevin: So, tell us, as far as your community involvement with your firm, do you have associations or groups that you help or reach out to?

Anne: We, in the last year, have attended and conducted presentations concerning the importance of estate planning with ALS support groups in both Colorado Springs and Denver. We reach out to MS, cancer, ALS, and any group that is interested in or wants us to come and speak about the importance of estate planning. We go do this at any time, usually Saturdays or evenings, just to get the message out and let people know that there are resources out there, that this process is easy.

Kevin: And what's the biggest challenge you're facing right now?

Anne: Convincing people that they need to get an estate plan. That is the number one challenge. People think, "I don't need it right now. I'm young." Or, "I don't want to think about passing. I don't want to think about it, period." And it's convincing people that whatever age you are, it's good to have an estate plan in place.

Kevin: So, it deals with things like guardianship and all that, if you have kids under 18?

Anne: Absolutely. Yes. Those are really important.

Kevin: So, if somebody didn't have that, how would the courts decide where the kids go?

Anne: If you don't have a will in place, everything has to go through the court, and that can take, a) months, and b) if you don't have something designated to a specific loved one, it opens the door for anyone in your life to challenge something, whether they want a piece of your jewelry or your car or your house. They can go to the court and say, "Jerry promised me that car." And if you don't have a will in place with your wishes, the court may give Jerry your car and that may not have been what you wanted.

Kevin: So, a will is a piece of the overall estate plan?

Anne: Correct. It's just one piece.

Kevin: Okay. What's the best advice you've ever received, Anne?

Anne: To be honest, if you want something done right, you should look into doing it yourself. Hindsight is 20-20. And you have to be your own advocate.

Kevin: That's great. That's really good. Yeah, nobody cares more than you do, right? About the things that are important to you.

Anne: Absolutely.

Kevin: What would you like to share that I haven't asked you?

Anne: I think there are many parts to planning for your future. It's not just estate planning; that's a big part of it, but it's also planning financially. It's having insurance in place and maybe having long-term care insurance in place. There's so much that you need to plan for and be aware of, because your future is coming and things are going to happen that you don't foresee. It's just so important to plan now.

Kevin: Where can our audience go to learn more about you?

Anne: We have a website: www.ccrjlaw.com. We have a lot of information in the Estate Planning section or in the News/Blogs section on estate planning. You can also reach us over the phone.

Kevin: What's your phone number?

Anne: Our number is 303-572-4200.

Kevin: Thank you so much, Anne.

Anne: Thank you.

CHAPTER 10

John Diak

John Diak is Principal and Client Wealth Manager at Oatley & Diak LLC in Parker, where he assists clients through many lifestyle changes such as business downturns, retirement planning, divorce, the death of a spouse, and family estate issues, among others. He is a Certified Financial Planner CFP® and a Certified Divorce Financial Analyst®, and has been repeatedly recognized by 5280 Magazine as one of "Denver's Top Wealth Managers."

John has more than 20 years of personal and corporate finance experience. Before becoming a Certified Financial Planner, he was CFO and owner of a professional service company. He is a member of the Rotary Club of Cherry Creek Valley and the Financial Coaching Ministry of Southeast Christian Church. He has also donated professional services to local organizations including Praying Hands Ranch, Parker Senior Center, Double Angel Ballpark and the Miller Safety Center.

Kevin: I'm with financial planner John Diak, CFP® from Parker, Colorado. So, tell me the name of and about your firm.

John: Oatley and Diak, LLC. We are a financial planning firm.

Kevin: Where did you grow up? Where are you from?

John: Originally, I was born in Philadelphia, Pennsylvania. I moved to Parker, Colorado in 1983. I graduated from a local high school, Ponderosa High School, and have been in Parker ever since.

Kevin: That's a beautiful place to live, for sure. At one point, Douglas County was the fastest growing county in the country.

John: Yes. I've seen significant growth. Previous to my career in financial planning, I was a shareholder at a professional service company (land surveying). This afforded me a chance to participate very intimately with the growth of Douglas County.

Kevin: So, tell us about your childhood. What was it like? What did your parents do?

John: Childhood was a typical suburban childhood, growing up in the Philadelphia area. My father was an accountant for Arthur Young and my mom was a homemaker. I spent a lot of time with my mom. She was very active in giving her time back to the community and creating relationships. My father gave me his talent for numbers. He would bring over his clients/peers and allow me to sit down with them and observe his discussions on high-level financial matters such as entity structure, tax efficiency and tax planning. It was a fascinating perspective for a child. I would listen and then afterward I would ask questions. These discussions really fostered my interest in the financial arena.

Kevin: From your mom you got the philanthropy side, or the giving back, and from your dad you got the entities, business and numbers?

John: Mom was the person who gave me my moral compass. She was the person I saw giving her time to local organizations, being there for friends and neighbors and creating a social agenda so we never were disconnected from those people or organizations that were important to both the community and us.

Dad was an analytic. He was a brilliant person when it came to numbers and communicating what was important through spreadsheets and other reporting methods. One thing I learned as the years progressed was that people really valued what he had to offer. He had a presence about him—integrity and the ability to find "right"—that people really appreciate. For me, that was something to aspire to as I grew up.

Kevin: Absolutely. What made you want to pursue a career in financial planning?

John: Looking back to my childhood, numbers just seemed to come easily. When I was attending Colorado State University, the logical step was to go into business school. At that time, you couldn't directly get into business school. You had to take some pre-requisite classes. In the interim, I signed up for a few classes that my older sister took on her track to becoming a teacher—human development and family studies classes. Those classes really resonated with me. Learning about the human lifecycle and what social implications each phase of life was dealing with was very insightful. I pursued a dual major in Business Finance and Human Development and Family Studies.

Upon graduating in the early '90s, I wanted to help people with their financial matters, but the financial services industry seemed very transactional. As I interviewed with a few local mutual funds and wire houses, I didn't find what I was looking for. So, I joined a local professional service company. For the first 13 years of my working life, I was fortunate to be a participant in building most major construction projects in the Colorado region. My father-in-law was the one who rekindled my desire to help people financially. He asked me to join the family practice in 2006.

Kevin: What year did you open up Oatley and Diak?

John: Oatley and Diak was formed in 1998 in response to my father-in-law's tax and corporate clients who wanted personalized investment advice.

Kevin: What do you wish you had known when you started, that you know now?

John: Financial services is about aligning your business with who you are as a person and getting the message out. It took a number of years to get to a point where I understood that principle and made those connections to further the business. I'm still learning how to do this better.

Kevin: What would you say is your sound bite or your unique selling proposition—what they call USP. How do you distinguish yourself? There are lots of financial planners, right?

John: We're a local family firm that has great knowledge and wisdom and can provide sound advice and guidance throughout your life. We have people within this practice at different phases of the life cycle and their different perspectives allow us to understand client challenges—both financial and non-financial.

Kevin: And life changes, doesn't it? And then their needs change.

John: Yes. I have to marry the financial to the ever-changing non-financial goals and objectives and determine what steps to take in order to achieve. We work together to create a personalized road map and come together in order to measure progress. The key is open and honest client communication. I'm 100 percent available for clients. I can be with them when they have questions. I can be the counselor, the therapist, their champion, and their friend.

Kevin: You wear lots of different hats.

John: I do. Every client relationship is different and each client has different goals. It's one of those things that all comes down to what do you want out of life? How do you want to live your life? I can't tell you. But I can hopefully create that conduit in which you can achieve most of your goals and objectives.

Kevin: Let's talk for a minute about seniors because the book is geared to helping seniors approaching or in retirement. And you know there are lots of twists and turns as they are in that stage of life. What are some things that you do as a firm to help the senior population?

John: My role with the senior population goes beyond the firm's limits. One of my civic commitments is to provide senior services. Currently, I serve my town of Parker as a board member on the Denver Regional Council of Governments (DRCOG). It's very challenging to keep up with the increasing need and demand for services and here, in Douglas County, we're at ground zero of the senior population in growth in Colorado.

Kevin: So, a lot of seniors are moving here, is what you're saying?

John: A lot of seniors are moving here, but also a lot of seniors are just aging in place. Even though the new housing has attracted a younger demographic, there are people who have been in their house for 30-plus years and are quite content. These people want and need more senior offerings, park and recreational opportunities, cultural events or just areas to gather to visit with friends.

My position at DRCOG allows me to understand the challenges seniors have getting access to a network of care. DRCOG oversees the Area Agency on Aging (AAA) that facilitates various senior services. The AAA allows a senior to connect with advocates in order to find service providers or non-profits that can assist with the many challenges that confront the senior population.

Kevin: Many seniors don't know where to go or whom to trust.

John: Correct. Everything is so fractionalized, especially if you're an older individual. You may or may not have a base of family or friends in the area. There are many non-financial issues to make sure there's awareness of. It's very challenging. As a financial planner, I utilize my knowledge in various areas of service offerings in order to help my clients. The senior citizen client values having a person that understands their challenges and that they can call for assistance in addressing the many challenges life presents.

Kevin: That's great. So, John, what are the highlights of your position as a financial planner?

John: Helping people—defining who they are financially, what they want out of life and reconciling to create an actionable plan. I'm a results person. I like to see other people succeed. I like to see people get educated and understand the process. To be a small part of that in somebody's life, so they can achieve as much as possible of what they want, is very rewarding. In my financial practice, I'm a fiduciary; it's putting your client's interests above your own. I have always acted in that manner—personally and professionally. I just want to see people succeed, and encourage them along the way. I want them to live the life they want to live. That's as rewarding as it could possibly get.

Kevin: That's great. So, you mentioned aging in place. Most people want to stay in their home for as long as they can.

What are some ways that you help seniors age in place, or stay in their homes for as long as they can?

John: It goes back to resource awareness. I'm a financial planner, I know a lot about financial matters, but when it comes to the non-financial matters and services, it's about trying to discover and learn about the various services in home care. I constantly learn and understand what's available to not only me, but to everybody else as a value to my clients. Then, I go out and actively seek those people and provide that information to them. It's very difficult for seniors to understand what services are out there.

Kevin: It's overwhelming for them, isn't it?

John: It is. As a financial professional, I think my purpose is greater. I view myself as more of a holistic financial person, somebody who will try to help you in matters that are also non-financial. As you go through life, there are challenges you have to overcome. I've helped clients through divorce. If they're having challenges, I refer them to a therapist. That's sort of what I view as my value added. I try and offer those non-financial options to them at the right time so they can consider their choices.

Kevin: That's awesome. So, we talked a second ago about how there are all these resources and it's overwhelming for seniors. Who do they trust and all those kinds of things? What are some of the most common mistakes you see seniors make as they approach or are in retirement?

John: A recent article indicated a person's cognitive peak at 53 to 55 with consistently sharp declines every year after. It's almost a reverse bell curve. Some of the mistakes I see seniors making is not aligning themselves with trusted advisors and not creating a plan early enough. Planning early is the best practice. If you don't have trusted relationships with attorneys, accountants and financial advisors, abuse could come into play. In Colorado, the state legislator passed a bill providing financial advisors the ability to report potential financial abuse without recourse. I applaud that. The senior population is one of parents and grandparents. I respect those people; those people have sacrificed to make my life better. I hold those people in high regard and I don't think that anybody should take advantage of those people who have given so much to my generation and all those generations following.

Kevin: Absolutely. Are there specific things you do to help solve these problems? You mentioned about planning earlier, and that kind of thing.

John: I want to be an advocate for seniors and vulnerable populations. I like working with people in crisis to assist in creating order. I work with seniors who are widowed or divorced.

I network with local agencies who deal with people in crisis in an attempt to be knowledgeable when someone is referred. I let people know that I'm always available to help or to assist. I got involved in a financial literacy program at a local church, probably six or seven years ago, and it's just great to sit down and give back.

Kevin: We did that at our church, too.

John: Whether it's sitting down with somebody who doesn't know how to budget or can't afford their rent, or on the other extreme, somebody who's five years away from retirement and they've done everything themselves, but they just kind of want to make sure they're okay. There's a whole lot of in-between, but just to be a resource and to try and say, "Listen, I'm here to help." My practice is, "If you just need to talk, let's talk. If I can help you and solve all your problems in one meeting, that's great. I'm glad to do it. If there's something more that you want me to do, we can create a relationship going forward. Let's talk about that." People are kind of refreshed with that perspective. Generally, the first meeting is, "Here's who I am, here's what my issues are." But there are just some people who are at a point that they just need some direction. It could be a very minor thing, but in their world, it's very major. They don't know where to go, and they beat themselves up so much. I just want to be available to try to align their figures and concerns and maybe give them a little bit of direction.

Kevin: John, what do you like best about your practice, your business?

John: Being a part of a family practice is something that's rewarding. It seems like every business entity I've been a part of is one of the family. Honoring our family values, we treat everyone like family—give them good service and provide them with the guidance to fulfill their personal goals. Personally, I enjoy using my past experience to enhance and better the client. I was a businessman first and foremost. I ran a mid-size professional service firm. I worked on large-scale infrastructure projects, and I have a different perspective. I'm not a sales person. I know the lifecycle of humans and I know how to financially manage an operation and an organization, and how to marry those two. I've heard people use the term "personal CFO" before. I am well versed to do that, both from an individual and small business standpoint, based on my skill set. Doing that for people is very rewarding as well.

Kevin: What product or technique or service do you offer that you wish more of your clients knew about?

John: I don't know if it's a product or an offering, I think it's more of the quarterly meeting or just the regular meeting. There are some people in the practice who don't take advantage of that. That's the time to develop and maintain relationships. The financial service industry has changed over the last 20 to 30 years from being a sales transaction-based industry to being one of relationship-based, what I call, "hand-holding." People want others to listen, to understand, to know them, and to help them. We still have people who don't value sitting down and having intermittent talks.

I get value as the relationship evolves. An hour meeting usually is spent with a mature client who understands and has been with us for a while. We talk about everything but finances for the first 50 minutes—you know, "How are the kids? Here's what's happening in my life." I get value out of that because those are the things that tie back to their goals and objectives. I'm trying to assure that they are achieving what they truly want in life. They also tell me about their family, so again, there could be some opportunities there.

I sat down with one client and we talked and it seemed like she was kind of concerned about her family. When it came time to make her required minimum distribution (RMD), she goes, "But I don't know what to do with this, I just should probably invest this back in the stock market." I go, "I don't think you should. I think you should maybe be investing that in your family. You spent 45 minutes telling me how each of your adult children has some challenges and it's been weighing on you."

It's important to be a cheerleader, and to make those connections back to what they told me was important back in the beginning. Trying to be a guide to someone's financial world and to ensure that their goals and objectives are being adhered to is kind of nice at times. Because at times, I don't have to talk about return on investment, I have to talk about, "Remember you told your late husband you would go to Europe. That was one of your goals, and even though he is no longer here, you should honor that. You should honor him". Being that facilitator and creating awareness on personal goals is very rewarding and special.

Kevin: John, think about a recent senior client that you helped. Tell us about their situation, what they were trying to accomplish and how you were able to help them.

John: I am developing a client right now; she came six months after her husband passed away. They both had jobs, did the right thing, but they had never gone through a process to sort of inventory their financial assets. She had a whole lot of paperwork, so we sat down and went through it. It took a couple meetings. She was still getting over the passing of her husband, but we also needed to understand what needed to get done. Spending the time helped to understand what she had—if there was anything out there that we needed to know about to either pay off in terms of bills, or any accounts that just weren't really relevant. There were a couple accounts which only gave annual statements. We organized her financial picture and then had conversations regarding looking forward. "What do you want your life to look like? How much do you spend now? What's your budget?"

She went through all of that information while still thinking about her late husband. We finally got through it and it came to a point where we really knew what she needed. We're making some adjustments to kind of consolidate her holdings, to kind of keep it simple for her. I'm going to be that one phone call point-of-contact to make things simple.

She's a little bit vulnerable now, she's bringing in these offerings and she's getting emails and phone messages about guaranteed rates of return, and she doesn't know what to do. So, it's great to get that information and to walk her through, and say, "Okay here's what this is. Or if you want to pursue this, let's pursue it together so we understand." To get somebody who wasn't the financial dominant in the relationship into a position where she understands their financial picture is very empowering. I'm providing her the information she needs to make good decisions.

Kevin: So really when you boil it down, everybody kind of wants the same thing, right? Do I have enough money to live the life I want to live, to accomplish the things I want to do? I don't know how long I'm going to live, so I want to be sure I don't run out of money. Isn't that kind of what everybody at the end of the day wants? And you're kind of helping them navigate that.

John: Pre-retirement, it's obviously different phases. If you're young, you just want to make money—as much as you can—and you want to enjoy your lifestyle. But you're also going to have an eye towards the future, towards retirement. As you get closer to retirement, you sort of have to take stock and say, "Okay, how am I going to transition or get myself ready for retirement? What choices do I have to make?"

It's more about awareness. It's almost like flying in a plane. People want to get off the ground as quick as possible, because they want to live their life. They want to get out of high school, they want out of college, so all of a sudden, they take off. And take off is full of wonder and you're going fast, climbing, and all of a sudden you get to that point where you're cruising and, hopefully, doing the right things. The challenge is to avoid turbulence during the flight—overspending or misallocation of finances.

People are at different phases, but what I do is recognize who they are and devote realistic goals and objectives so they can live the life they want to live. If they're unrealistic, that's the hard part, because I then have to say, "Okay, you cannot achieve those," or "You have to work longer in order to hopefully achieve those." So, it's a delicate balancing act, but if you have somebody who understands their priorities, "What do you want to do in your life? What do you value? What's important and what do you have? And can you sustain that through retirement?" it is easier.

Kevin: Let's talk for a minute about the ideal client. What's an ideal client for you?

John: My ideal client is one that has a passion to better themselves, create clarity in their lives and align what is important in their non-financial life with their finances. People that have a passion to be better, want to learn and understand the value that an advisor such as myself, or an attorney, or a CPA, can provide.

Kevin: What's the first step you'd like them to take?

John: I want to establish a relationship. I have a general conversation to get to know who they are, what is important to them and to identify some of the challenges they currently have in their lives. The person also gets a chance to determine if I'm someone they would like to work with. I want them to find somebody that they can work and can connect with on a long-term basis. I encourage them to talk to other advisors and make an educated decision. I tell them they should look for certain things—the Certified Financial Planner (CFP®) credential and somebody who truly has your interest at heart. I give them unbiased literature that says, "Here are some questions that you should ask other people." It doesn't lead back to me. It provides the groundwork so the person can interview an advisor and know what to ask, so that they can make a decision.

Kevin: How do your ideal clients find you, typically?

John: Generally, it's a referral from a professional, client or friend. Working in the community that I grew up in for the last 30-plus years, word of mouth is a part of client acquisition. I'm trying to increase my social media presence. I have hired a marketing consultant to get my online information aligned. But, quite honestly, the people that come are generally people that know someone that I know, or have seen me at an event and they were interested.

Kevin: What's the biggest challenge you're facing right now?

John: The changing regulatory environment is becoming a challenge. I believe it's changing in our favor, being a registered investment advisor (RIA). The fiduciary standard rule is one that we have subscribed to since day one, but the industry has not operated on the principle of putting client's interests above your own interests.

Another challenge is managing client expectations. We are a comprehensive planning firm that relies on creating and executing a unique client plan. When things are good in the equity markets, conservative clients want returns that are inconsistent with the plan. They want a return greater than their risk tolerance. It goes back to the plan, the roadmap at the beginning. If we do it right, we have defined goals and objectives and we defined the risk tolerance so we know how to invest.

Kevin: What's the best advice you've ever received?

John: There are a few words of wisdom that I attribute to my father, "There's no shortcut to right," and, "Put your head down, do good work, and people will find you." You just don't know how long something is going to take, but do it to the best of your ability and deliver a good product for your client. If done consistently, clients will talk and others you can help will follow.

Another bit of wisdom comes from my father-in-law, "Find something that you love to do and are passionate about, and do it." Be purposeful and passionate in everything you do. This will show through to others. I think my father-in-law and my father had similar advice using different words—do the best you can for people. It's not about yourself and if you can help other people, we all win.

Kevin: What would you like to share that I haven't asked you?

John: I think seniors are in a critical situation right now. From a federal level, we don't have a whole lot of funding to take care of their needs. We're living longer, and we're consumers, so we haven't saved enough. We need to figure out a way to take care of that gap. We, as a society, need to look inward at the family and say, "Hey, what can the family do to help?" I was raised where family and family-like friendships are very important and you help each other out. My hope is that we can find a way to get back to those thoughts and feelings.

If there's somebody in need or a certain age demographic in need, we can figure out a way, together, to resolve that or to at least limit their exposure to later in life challenges. In the past, churches and neighborhood organizations have provided great success at identifying and addressing community challenges.

We still need some help from the government regarding health care, but if we work together and ask, "How can we make this better?" we will be able to resolve many challenges. We just need to come together as Americans, as people, and try to define what the issue is and work towards resolving that issue. It's as simple as that.

Kevin: How can people find you? Where can they go to learn more about you?

John: People can connect through email (jdiak@oatleydiak.com) or the Oatley & Diak website (www.oatleydiak.com). The website provides a greater perspective on how we operate and what we can do for a person, family or corporation.

Kevin: Thank you John, I appreciate it.

John: You bet.

CHAPTER 11

Rick Sutton

Rick Sutton is an insurance broker and registered representative at Sutton & Associates, LLC, which he founded in 1984. He specializes in employee benefits, executive and family insurance coverage, 401(k) rollovers, retirement analysis including Social Security and Medicare, and the consequences of an extended care event.

Rick has a long track record of community service, including the Kiwanis Club, where he's a past president, Arapahoe High School Key Club sponsor, and Junior Achievement business consultant. He's also a longtime youth baseball and football coach, high school wrestling official, and sexual abuse prevention and disclosure advocate and speaker.

Kevin: I'm talking to Rick Sutton. He does Medicare and long-term care. Rick, tell us a little bit about yourself. Where did you grow up?

Rick: I'm from Omaha, Nebraska. I came to Colorado because my mother married a GI at Fort Carson. I went to high school there, and then went to college up in Gunnison to be a teacher and coach. I changed careers after seven and a half years to be an investment advisor and insurance guy back in 1977. And throughout all these years I've maintained numerous contacts with kids. Speaker, volunteer, Kiwanis, whatever. That's pretty much who I am.

Kevin: Awesome. What did your parents do?

Rick: My dad wrapped cable with plastic at Western Electric. My mom was a hair stylist.

Kevin: So, you're here in the Denver area, the DTC (Denver Tech Center). How long have you been focusing on long-term care and Medicare? And what made you want to focus on that part of the business?

Rick: I've been doing it about 25 years. Why? That's an interesting question. What made me want to focus? Protecting assets, protecting one's retirement, the aspect of leveraging five cents on the dollar. For instance, the cost of premium for long-term care policy versus the cost of being in a facility was easily demonstrable. It was fairly priced back in the day, 10, 15, 20 years ago. Obviously, people hung onto their policies. The insurance companies had underpriced them, thinking that the people would let their policy lapse when they didn't need any more. But the people who purchased long-term care from yours truly intended on being around when they were on the verge of not being around. It's crazy that the insurance industry missed that one. That perception. The purpose of purchase, perception. So, the price has gone up. It's less attractive to people, but it's still around. Bill Gates and the guy from Omaha both have long-term care policies in spite of their billions. Leveraging dollars.

Kevin: Good to know. Rick, what do you wish you had known when you started with Medicare long-term care, that you now know?

Rick: That's a difficult question to answer, because what I've always done is listen to a client. "What's important to you? What keeps you awake at night?" And then being aware of solutions, either products or conversations that help people grasp the issue of extended care—which gives the possibility of not putting your loved ones in the position of having to fund your care, if you have it. So, what do I wish I would have known then? I'm not aware of something specific, but overall, I probably learned on the run.

Kevin: Tell us about some of the highlights of what you do.

Rick: I'm a salesperson who meets with different people every day on what they want to talk about. It is a constantly changing universe. You can't get bored in the business of meeting with people and trying to assuage their worries and concerns about their retirement. That lends itself to when someone's 45, let alone when they're 65 or 70. And so, the Medicare thing is still operable in America for people that are approaching that age.

Kevin: That's awesome. One of the big things we find with seniors is that they want to stay in their home as long as they can. They want to age in place. What are some things that you do to help them do that?

Rick: What a long-term care policy will do is protect assets that are targeted and earmarked for retirement, travel, lifestyle, etc. It depends on the dollar. So, protecting assets for what they were intended for, namely retirement, as opposed to the unforeseen and regrettable expense of going into care, which can scare the daylights out of a lot of people. It's peace of mind. People worry about Medicare, but obviously, people are living a whole lot longer than our parents did. The gold watch, 30 years, retire at 65 and that means watch TV and sit on the veranda. Not anymore. I know the stats on how long people are supposed to live after they get to certain ages. If you pass the threshold of 65, you're going to live on average beyond 88 for men and 91 for women.

Kevin: What are some of the most common mistakes you see seniors make as they approach or are in retirement?

Rick: They get too conservative in their investment portfolios. There's still too much time that they need to take advantage of whatever market. One can be conservative, but burying it in the backyard like Grandma used to do—those people from the '30s hid their money in the basement. That's a common mistake, viewing that I've got my money now I just want to keep it. It needs to be in play to some degree. It's a matter of percentages. Is 20 percent of your money at play in what's going on in the world or 50 percent? Somebody like me with high-risk tolerance would be 60 to 70 percent at play, 30 percent locked up. My spouse would be 70 to 80 percent the other way. People get a little bit too conservative too soon because their parents only lived to 68, but they're going to live a lot longer.

Kevin: Okay. How do you help solve those problems?

Rick: Well getting people to think through considering plans A, B, C and D. What plans do you have in the event of an extended-care event for yourself or your spouse? What is it that you want to spend your money on? When do you want to start drawing it? Do you have obligations to children, to your own parents that will affect your portfolio? What you've earned? What you've saved? Getting people to think through, to have a plan. To develop a plan, whatever it involves.

Kevin: So, if somebody doesn't have a plan, what are their options when it comes to long-term care?

Rick: Whatever hits you in the face, will hit you in the face. As you get older to 60, 65, and 70 certainly, your expectations for acquiring long-term care become more and more limited due to preexisting conditions. So, the trick is, even though you don't want to be in a nursing home or a facility, planning and putting money aside for that eventuality is necessary. Otherwise you could devastate and wipe out everything you've strived to accumulate and to have for a legacy to pass on perhaps.

Kevin: So, really people have maybe four choices, right? They can self-fund. They can go live with their kids. They can go into a state-run facility. Or they can transfer the risk, is what you're suggesting.

Rick: To an insurance policy. There's a fifth option, though, and that would be to allocate a particular asset for being able to be liquidated. Let's say a piece of property of some kind, or maybe that mutual fund. But it voids the actual leveraging of dollars at extraordinarily discounted cost to be able to fund it. If someone had a relative who's gone into care, they will, in fact, be more receptive to discussing it. Whatever your plan is, it may be the purchasing or transferring your risk to an insurance company. But if you haven't thought about it and the day comes when there's a need, you're not likely to have the capacity to react well to it.

Kevin: I saw a stat that something like two-thirds of Americans are going to need some form of care and less than 10 percent have something in place. Does that sound right?

Rick: Those are good accurate numbers. For a married couple, it's 68 percent likely for one of them to be in care before their demise.

Kevin: You know, we have auto insurance. We have homeowners' insurance. We have health insurance. Some people have life or disability insurance. Why do you think there's so much resistance about long-term care insurance?

Rick: It's a place the average person doesn't want to go to—the idea of thinking about it when you're 50 or 55. The product has been sold as long-term care insurance. Well, who names something the one thing that people don't want to be in? So, extended care is a euphemism. It is another way.

But most people will be in home care. Most people will be receiving care in the home. A nurse comes in two to three times a week. I recall stats that the average person who goes into care is receiving in-home care four and a half years prior to ever going into a facility. As you probably know, supposedly 40 percent of all people in extended care receiving assistance with the basic activities of daily living are under age 60. It's not because they got too old. It's because they skied into a tree drunk. They drove a car and had an accident and need assistance. Let me go on with that a little bit.

The question is whether you're going to have options and care that are appropriate, affordable, etc., as the baby boomers mature. There are 10,000 a day turning 65. The ticket is to have a plan, and hopefully one that's leveraged in terms of insurance product to transfer your risk. The whole purpose of insurance of every kind we could discuss, is to transfer one's risk of something bad happening that would mess with your financial and physical well-being.

Kevin: So, if somebody needs to go into a facility, what is it per month today?

Rick: That varies all over the country, but in Colorado we're approaching $90,000 a year for a semi-private room. That translates to about $7,500 per month. But facilities vary enormously. Assisted living is about two-thirds of that. Assisted living means you may need somebody to watch you take a shower, maybe help occasionally getting down to dinner in a wheelchair, but you don't need care full-time from a caregiver. Obviously, there are different facilities that cost a wide range in the metropolitan area. Limon's going to be one-half of that cost. But are you able to pay for some of it, so that your assets can supplement? It's all a matter of transferring one's risk—if you perceive you have a risk because of the occurrence of an event.

And considering that in 68 percent of couples, one of them is going to be in care, it's a probability. And I happen to know that only one person in 1,200 has ever had their home burn down, and one in 240 has had their car totaled. And yet, all of us have homeowners and car insurance. Most of us have life insurance and we're all going to die, but are we going to die young? Extraordinarily unlikely. But you're probably going to go someplace where you don't want to be. What are the consequences of that? The whole question is, what are the consequences of an unwanted, unforeseen, God forbid, extended care situation?

Kevin: That's great information. Rick, what do you like best about your business?

Rick: My business is something that everybody needs to have a conversation about. I have clients who refer me to people they care about. If I want a wall or patio built on my property, getting a recommendation from a friend who says, "That guy will show up and do the job with integrity," is gold in this world. My whole business is about referrals. My clients refer me to other people that they're having cocktails with and something from Medicare comes up. So that's what's attractive about it, people networking.

Kevin: Is there a product or a technique or a service you offer you wish more senior clients knew about?

Rick: The service I render is that I know a fair amount about the subject at hand. Medicare, Social Security and the extended care, long-term care business. I know the landscape. And people basically engage me because they feel inadequate. So, it lends itself to bringing together those who need a service and those who can provide it. Which is myself for this.

Kevin: Okay. Tell us about a recent client that you helped. What was their situation? What were they hoping to accomplish and how did you help them?

Rick: Well, I typically look at my old-school appointment book to recall a particular client on a particular issue. But let's go with a couple I was referred to. Call them Rick and Dee. She's eight years younger than him. We sign up for a Medicare Advantage Plan. But it turns out there's a question relative to his eligibility, because he waited until age 67 to sign up for Part B, and he failed to check his messages within the seven-day limit for being able to get it. So that insurance company, I won't say their name, wiped out the application. They voided it, because they didn't get an answer to a question. And the only reason we learned about it is because I called in to see where it was in the process.

So, we meet again. He drives over to my place with his two grandkids. And I do the task. I complete the task, because people don't have a clue typically about how to interact with the government relative to something that a lot of people take for granted. That's an added value with me.

Kevin: Rick, who's an ideal client for you?

Rick: Those are all outstanding questions, by the way. An ideal client is someone who is in their mid-60s or approaching the Medicare thing, and they want to be oriented as to their options—and somebody they trust, a friend or family member, has referred them to me. I'm bringing expertise to the table. And at some point in that conversation, hopefully in the first five or 10 minutes, they recognize credibility. I'm gratified by the fact that I can bring solutions to the table for someone who doesn't have the confidence that they can sort it out themselves. We have expertise, and being able to demonstrate it is gratifying, whether you're a major-league baseball player or any profession. You're supposed to be able to do that.

Kevin: Yes. What's the first step you'd want these ideal clients to take?

Rick: Just call me.

Kevin: How do your ideal clients find you? You mentioned you do a lot of work by referral?

Rick: It's virtually all referral. Now this past week, I sent out about 60 or 70 old-school letters about Medicare to existing clients with long-term care who are approaching 65 or already are. Let's say they have a Medicare supplement policy that's aging, and these companies slip in rate increases that the client thinks are just normal. These insurance companies don't inform people like me, because they don't want us to mess with their relationship. So, we'll check, "What are you being charged right now? And is that in line with the market?" It's a way to stay in touch with clients. We'll see if I hear back from any of them. But I'm staying in touch. They know I'm conscious of them.

Kevin: What's the biggest challenge you're facing right now with your business?

Rick: The absence of many carriers that want to do long-term care insurance. They've dropped out—the Hancocks and numerous others. There are a few that are still committed. But the Medicare piece is a matter of having resources to solve people's problems. I've never pursued the carrier that pays the best commission, because they're likely to be having rate increases later. I like to refer to them as gorillas. I use the ones that doctors know and clients recognize that are more likely to be stable.

Kevin: What's the best advice you've ever received?

Rick: I'm going to say something along the lines of, "The number one value system I have is, to do what you say you're going to do or don't do it. Do it right. Keep your word. Keep your agreement." That's advice I pass on to young people I work with, because it is such a differentiator in our universe.

I will ask people, "When somebody told your grandma that they were going to fix something, do something or send something, how many times out of 10 could she assume that it was going to be accomplished?" And the answer is almost always nine and a half.

Okay, how about today? Whatever their age, it drops below five. I ask that question a lot. We live in a universe where someone you need to rely on may or may not have that value system. What does that mean about our society? So, the best advice I ever got was to always keep your word. Do what you say you're going to do.

Kevin: Absolutely. What would you like to share that I haven't already asked you?

Rick: We all have careers. We each have an expertise. We have what we do to make a living, but I'm most proud of what I do with kids. Volunteer stuff, my Kiwanis Club. I see economically disadvantaged fifth graders twice a week. I also take care of their garden. I was voted into that because I'm a gardener. At Arapahoe High School I was the Key Club sponsor for 27 or 28 years. It's a matter of doing the old payback thing.

Kevin: Pay it forward.

Rick: Yes, that's a phrase I never liked, but that's what I mean. There's a whole lot more that we're supposed to be doing for our communities than just making a living. I'm most proud of what I do when I'm not selling stuff.

Kevin: Where can our audience go to learn more about you?

Rick: I have a website. www.TheTimberlineGroupLLC.com. Or call my work number, 303-347-2656.

Kevin: Thank you Rick.

CHAPTER 12

Kathy Chapman

Kathy Chapman is president of Colorado Senior Insurance. She helps people plan for the future and protect themselves in the present, with Medicare plans and long-term care insurance.

She has experienced first-hand the need for long-term care, serving as a caregiver for her elderly mother, who has Alzheimer's disease.

In addition to working in this field, Kathy is also a board member of Colorado Healthcare Strategy Management, the state's only non-profit association serving all aspects of healthcare.

Kevin: We're talking to Kathy Chapman, who has Colorado Senior Insurance. Tell us a little bit about yourself. Where are you from originally?

Kathy: I'm from Binghamton, N.Y. I moved down to Tucson in 1976, to go to the University of Arizona because it was warm and sunny.

Kevin: How did you end up in Colorado?

Kathy: I visited a family member here, and I liked that the mountains were right next to a city with museums. And it wasn't too hot; it wasn't too cold. It was sunny, but also cloudy, and there weren't a lot of creepy, crawly bugs. Colorado really doesn't have many insects. It's amazing.

You can leave your windows open and not be bitten to death.

Kevin: That's true. So, tell us about your childhood.

Kathy: I was one of six children. I was the oldest girl, and I had to take care of my brothers and sisters, because my parents worked. I had a nice extended family. My grandmother, my great-grandmother, my aunt and uncle, and their two children were there. We would have Sunday dinner together probably every other week, because it was someone's birthday or a holiday. My mom would cook a big meal. We had the kid's table and we had the grownups table. It was a very nice life because Binghamton is blue collar. People would get off the boats in New York City, and say, "Which way EJ?" which is Endicott Johnson, a shoe factory. When I was growing up there was IBM, there was Singer Link, there was the Endicott Johnson factory, and there were a couple other factories.

In fact, it's still a factory town, except that most of the factories have left. Our town consisted of Irish, Polish, and Italian people. We were all equal. Everybody got along, and everybody helped each other. It was really a great place to live. The only problem was, it was always kind of raining. It was very similar to Seattle, or I would say Portland. It was very similar there, because it's a river valley. But, everybody was nice and everybody helped each other. I loved the '70s. I thought it was great.

Kevin: What kind of work did your parents do?

Kathy: My dad worked for the city; he drove a garbage truck, and my mom worked in a factory. She made bellows, so she would literally stand up all day, take a big pile of plastic, line it up, make it into a square, and then she would press this machine, and they would cut the plastic to make bellows. A bellow is something like an accordion, so if you have a corkscrew type drill, or something like that, you need to put this bellow on it to keep the dust off. It's called a dust bellow. When manufacturing was big, they had a lot of machines, which needed dust bellows. Mom would work all day, then come home and cook us a full dinner every night. We had eight people in our family. She did the laundry and the cooking, and we did all the cleaning. It was nice to grow up in a nice extended family. People are really nice there, and everybody just helps each other.

Kevin: So, what made you want to pursue a career in the Medicare business?

Kathy: I actually never wanted to be a Medicare broker. But I love it. I went to school for a business degree, because I wasn't set up for any other things. I like the competitive part of business, the independence, and the variety. I received a business degree from the University of Arizona, and actually started in the cable TV industry in advertising. I wasn't selling advertising; I was working for someone who was setting up all of the cable television advertising departments. I was working for Warner AMEX, before it became Times Mirror. I was an administrative person; it was a new position. This was in Columbus, Ohio, where we moved to be near my husband's family. I was hired as a temporary secretary. My boss asked me to create brochures and create the marketing packets. I would hire all of the administrative people, write the job descriptions, and then she would hire the managers. Then I started doing budgeting and forecasting, and I'd travel all over the United States. I was 25 years old.

It was a great job. It was so nice. I loved that job. Then I moved to selling advertising for an independent rep firm. I was only 30 years old, making $70,000. But then I got divorced, and the only company that would hire me was Farmers Insurance. I needed to have a flexible schedule because I was a single mom. I was a Farmers agent for about a year, and I realized I was probably paying more to work there buying leads, than what I was making in commissions. You had to buy leads every day, and you had to call those leads to generate sales.

So, I found a job at Kaiser Permanente where I would receive retirement and pension and health insurance. I worked in the individual insurance department for two years selling directly to consumers. I moved into Medicare because I knew when the Affordable Care Act went into effect, it was going to be a lot more work. I taught myself Medicare, moved up to Northern Colorado, and moved into an apartment. I developed Laramie County the first year, and then the second year I developed Weld County. So, I had both counties. I was driving 2,000 miles a month though. I'd come home on the weekends.

Kevin: Wow.

Kathy: But we got a new boss, and the new boss decreased our commissions, so I left Kaiser Permanente. I actually needed to, because I was taking care of my mom at that time. My mother had Alzheimer's disease. I thought I could care for her by myself. Alzheimer's patients are very restless and very nervous and do a lot of pacing and get up at night. For security reasons, I needed to watch my mom 24 hours a day. Even though she attended a day program, the evenings and weekends were very difficult for me to keep my mother safe. I had to take the knobs off the stove, lock all the cabinets, and make sure she did not leave the house.

I finally had to move her to a care community, where she lived for two years. She just passed away last August. But now, I'm able to work more full-time and concentrate on building my business. That's why I'm focusing more on long-term care and Medicare now. I want to really develop that business now that I have more time to do that. So that's my life.

Kevin: So, what do you wish you had known when you started, that you know now, regarding Medicare?

Kathy: Nothing within Medicare. But the thing I wish I had known about, is https://www.medicare.gov/ because it's a great website. When people call me, the first thing I ask is, "Who are your doctors? What are your hospitals? And what drugs do you take?" On the Medicare website, you can click on "find a plan," and then you enter your drugs into that system. As soon as you enter one drug, it makes a drug list, and the date you made that list. People should write down their drug list number, and the date that they made the drug list. Then enter drugs, dosages, and times of day you take the drugs. After you enter the information, choose your pharmacies. After you choose your pharmacy, click on "find a plan" at the top of the page. Then a person can compare Medicare Advantage Plans and Medicare drug plans. It shows you all the plans that will cover your drugs. That's the first thing you look at, which plans will cover your drugs.

Kevin: That's great.

Kathy: If your plan doesn't cover your drug, you're going to pay 100 percent out of pocket. When people work with brokers, or they buy online, or through a TV ad, they don't know if their drug is covered. Representatives don't ask seniors about their drugs. So, the first step if you want to see if your drug is covered, is to look at the middle column and there will be a "yes." After you see that your drug is covered, you look to the left column, the first column, and then you see how much your drugs will cost per year, including the premium. At the top of the choices is the lowest amount you will pay for your drugs, including the deductible. Drug costs can be from $200 a month to $3,000 a month. If a person wants a Medicare Supplement plan, they need to purchase a stand-alone Medicare drug plan. If someone wants a Medicare Advantage plan, follow the same process to determine which Medicare Advantage plan is the right plan each year.

People can change Medicare drug plans and Medicare Advantage plans every year from October 15 through December 7. It is a law that everyone on Medicare must be enrolled in a drug plan, otherwise, there will be a lifetime penalty. If your drug is not covered on your plan choice, then you do not want to consider that plan, because you will have to pay 100 percent for the drug.

Kevin: Great information. What do you like best about your position?

Kathy: I really help people. I keep them healthy. I save them money. I protect them.

Kevin: One of the things we see with seniors is they want to stay in their home as long as possible, age in place. What do you do to help seniors age in place?

Kathy: Well, I talk to them about who's going to care for them. Number one, Medicare does not cover any custodial or personal care. A lot of times, seniors are pretty healthy, and they can take their own medications. However, they might need help with getting out of bed, using the toilet, transferring, moving around the house, feeding themselves, or bathing. Those are things that people have a problem with, especially seniors with bathing, because a lot of them have tubs. So, they have falls. One of the main reasons a senior has to leave their home is because of falls. When my mom moved into our house, my husband took out the shower, and built a walk-in shower.

If there's one thing people can do, take out the tub, get a walk-in shower and then put handrails in there, and maybe even a little seat that folds down from the wall. That's the hardest thing for seniors, because they need to bathe.

They also need to feed themselves. Sometimes, people can't get to the grocery store. The things that I think are the hardest are bathing and feeding themselves, because they usually need assistance. Most seniors do not want to ask anybody to help them, and they don't want to leave their home. They're afraid to ask for help. That's what I think is the worst part for seniors.

Kevin: What are some of the most common mistakes you see seniors make as they approach or are in retirement?

Kathy: I think they give their kids money. That's the number one thing I don't like. They're helping their kids, and their kids aren't helping them. I see a lot of seniors. I deal mostly with people who are turning 65. I see them taking care of their elderly parents, so they might have quit their jobs and are not financially secure. Or if they're not taking care of a parent, then they're taking care of grandchildren, and they expect that the grandchildren will help them, or that their children will help them, but usually I see children living off their parents. That's the worst thing I see. I think the biggest problem for seniors is financial stability.

I think that's the worst problem for seniors, because they're not aware of their Medicare choices, their drug plan choices, and they're not aware of a lot of senior services that would help them save money. There's food assistance. There's utility assistance. There's home health assistance. There are all those programs. Even applying for Medicaid, if you're of a lower income, because it would pay for your co-pays if you were on a Medicare Advantage Plan. There's long-term Medicaid that would pay for financial assistance to keep your spouse in the home, and there's VA Aid and Attendance, which helps veterans and spouses pay for care in a home or community. When my mom qualified for VA Aid and Attendance, she received $900 per month and then she qualified for long-term Medicaid that paid for a day program, so the caretaker could go to work. They also paid for transportation to that day program.

When Mom went into a care community, they also paid for her nursing home care. It's hard to get into a care community if you have Medicaid. It does take some work, but it is possible. I think there are so many resources. I'm in a group called Senior Solutions, which is made up of people who work in the senior community. We have different people come in and talk about different senior programs, which could help seniors with vision, hearing, financial, even burial. Most people don't know about all of those programs. That's what I do. I tell a lot of people all of those things. I kind of interfere a little bit.

Kevin: Is there a product, technique, or service you offer, that you wish more of your senior clients knew about?

Kathy: I think I'm unique as a broker because a lot of brokers just know maybe one or two plans, but I represent all of the Medicare Advantage companies in Colorado. Right now, there are six of them. I represent Anthem, Aetna, Humana, United, Bright Health and refer to Kaiser Permanente. Rocky Mountain was just bought by United, so anyone on a Rocky Mountain plan will have a special open enrollment until February 15 to change to a new plan or qualify for a Medicare Supplement.

When I work with new customers, I always ask, "Do you have any group retiree benefits?" Because a lot of times, if you worked for companies like United Airlines, Chevron, or Lockheed, you might be eligible for some Medicare benefits through them, instead of buying it on your own. I think it's really important to look at all of your options, instead of just the person who came to your home, because all plans don't meet your needs. If your doctor doesn't accept it or if your drug is not accepted, then you don't want that plan.

Kevin: Without naming names, tell us about a recent client that you were able to help with Medicare. What was their situation? What were they hoping to accomplish? How did you deliver that?

Kathy: Well, I have this couple I met with yesterday. They just moved here from out of state. They have a Medicare Advantage Plan. When you have a Medicare Advantage Plan, you must get all of your service from people within the service area where you live. Even in Colorado, it depends on which Medicare Advantage Plan it is, because they want you to use a network.

Medicare pays the Medicare Advantage Plans a monthly fee to take care of you. When I worked at Kaiser, we had $800 per member, per month. They then go out and make a contract with different provider networks. That's why you have to live in your service area for six months of the year. So, these people just moved here. They're no longer in their service area; it's in another state. If they have to go and get any medical care, they only have an HMO. They have to go back to their service area to get that care, unless it's urgent or emergency care. When I met with them, they said, "Well, maybe we'll make a decision next month. I said, "I just want you to know, if you don't sign up by the end of this month and if you need any care, you will have to go back to where you were residing to get that care. Your Medicare Advantage Plan from out of state only covers urgent and emergency care when you are out of the area where you bought the plan." That's a really important thing. That's how I think I made a difference. I was also talking to them about what their needs were, and what they should go on. I think I help a lot of people, because sometimes people who aren't my customers call me about bills.

Also, one other very important thing about Medicare is that if you have a Medicare Advantage Plan, you have a monthly premium. A Medicare Advantage Plan is going to require you to use their doctors, hospitals, and purchase drugs, which are all covered on one plan for a low monthly premium as long as the person stays in network. It's like a United Healthcare Medicare Complete. That's the most popular plan. If you have one of those types of plans, when you go to the doctor, you pay that bill. You should never ever pay any other bills. There are so many billing errors.

I'm not going to mention a company name, but there's another company that sells a Medicare Advantage Plan, and their billing is horrible. People go to get outpatient surgery, and there are two things that could happen. On one plan—the company name I'm not going to mention—they often use an anesthesiologist that is not in network, so the patient has to pay for that out of pocket. That's a very bad thing. Also, they always send people bills, even when people don't owe them money. So, you have all these seniors paying bills when they do not owe the money. And they shouldn't be paying it.

Kevin: It sounds like it's easy for the patients to make that mistake.

Kathy: I want to give you another example. I have a 65-year-old client, referred to me by a financial advisor, and unfortunately, he had just developed a very serious form of cancer. He had to retire. He died a few weeks after he got his plan. When you turn 65, even though you're working, you automatically get your Medicare Part A, which is for when you're admitted in the hospital. That's what your Medicare tax pays out of your paycheck every month. When you look at your Medicare taxes you're paying for Hospital Part A. The patient only has to pay a small copay for a limited number of days for hospitalization. When a Medicare person is in the hospital, use your Medicare first, and then the group plan, Cobra, or Medicare will pay second.

So, this man called me to sign up for a Medicare plan. He

signed up for a Medicare Supplement Plan. Medicare Supplement pays the 20 percent that Medicare does not pay. Medicare Part A pays 80 percent. If you do not enroll in Medicare—even if you're out of the country—and you do not have any group employer insurance, you must enroll in Medicare within seven months of when you turn 65—three months before your birthday, the month of your birthday, and three months after. If you don't, you get a permanent late enrollment penalty.

Kevin: Oh, my.

Kathy: Many people are on individual plans and they don't realize that three months before they turn 65, they should go online and enroll in Medicare or call Social Security. You just go to the Medicare website to enroll. This particular gentleman had just retired, so he had Part A, and then he just signed up for Part B when I signed him up for Medicare. He had some procedures done because he had brain cancer. After he died, the hospital sent his widow a bill for $100,000. I told her, "Look, let me come by. Let me look at the bills. I'll tell you what's owed or not owed." She had all these bills all over the table. She showed me a $100,000 hospital bill. I reminded her that her husband had COBRA, so Cobra should pay the bill first and Medicare pays for the rest of the bill. I told her he does not have to pay the bill because Cobra and Medicare will pay the bill. I saved her $100,000.

That's a huge bill, but think about it, people get all these bills all the time. Part of my presentation to my customers is, if you're on a Medicare Advantage Plan and you receive any bills, then you do not pay because you already paid a copay when you used the medical service. You call up whoever billed you, and you tell them that they need to bill your Medicare Advantage Plan.

Kevin: That's awesome. What a great story. So, Kathy, who's an ideal client for you?

Kathy: First, let me say I hope my existing clients call me if they could refer friends or anyone else. An ideal client for me is anybody who is eligible for Medicare. Most of my clients are turning 65, because for 90 percent of the people, once you're on a plan, you do not change. The only reason you would change is if your plan doesn't cover your drug, and you're on a Medicare Advantage Plan. Of all the changes I did last year, 90 percent of them were just drug plans because their drugs weren't covered on the plan the next year. Not all plans cover all drugs. All plans charge different copays for the drugs, and each year the plan should tell you if you are not covered.

There's one more thing I'd like to say about drug plans. A lot of times people don't have to use their drug plan. They can either use one of the discount cards and pay cash, or use your Medicare Drug Plan. Sometimes it's actually a lot less expensive to use a drug discount card if you're on brand name drugs, than to use your drug plan because there's something called the *donut hole*, where you'll have to pay 41 percent once you reach a certain financial limit—until you get up to $4,700.

So, if you're on a couple of brand name drugs, it could cost you $3,000 per year. Also, ask the manufacturers of the drugs, "Do you have financial assistance programs to help people pay for their drugs?" Ask the pharmacy, when you pick up your prescription, if there's a discount card you can use there. Or bring your own discount card. Wal-Mart has a list of about a hundred drugs that people can get a 90-day supply for about a dollar to four dollars. There are a lot of resources for seniors, but the hardest part of Medicare for seniors is paying for their drugs.

Kevin: So, these ideal clients, what's the first step you'd want them to take?

Kathy: I like them to call me and ask me for information. They can reach me at 303-741-2726. They can also email me at

Kathy@coloradoseniorinsurance.com. That's my website, https://www.coloradoseniornsurance.com/. I'm licensed in Arizona, Colorado, Texas, New York, and Florida.

I think people need to look at their plan and see if there might be something better for them each year, because every plan has a zero dollar monthly premium plan. If they are struggling to pay for a Medicare Supplement, I recommend they choose a zero premium Medicare Advantage Plan for two reasons. One is to save money, because a lot of supplement plans increase their monthly premium each year as the person ages. Two, I recommend someone look at a Medicare Advantage Plan and be willing to change doctors. The great thing about a Medicare Advantage Plan is they do cover some Vision, Dental, and Hearing benefits that are not covered by Medicare in general. They also offer Silver Sneakers, which is a gym membership, which keeps people healthy.

People can change plans every year. They're welcome to call me. I help people every day, there's no charge because insurance companies pay me a commission.

Kevin: Okay, what's the best advice you've ever received?

Kathy: It was from my mom. I always say, "Quit your complaining or I'll give you something to complain about." Because, if you're from a large family, when we started complaining, she'd tell us, "Look, you have food, you have a house, what are you complaining about?" My mom was a role model because she'd go to work at 6:30 a.m. and get home at 4:30 p.m., and then she'd sit there and read a magazine. We would complain, "We're hungry, we're hungry," and she would tell us, "Let me relax for a while." Then each night she would cook us a full meal. So, I guess that's what I would say. "Quit your complaining," because really, we don't have much to complain about. That's what I'd say.

Kevin: Thank you, Kathy.

CHAPTER 13

Cory Davern

Cory Davern is Executive Vice President at America's Retirement Store, now known as Presidential Wealth Management. In addition to working with his own clients, Cory promotes the franchise across Colorado and nationally, hires and develops financial advisors for the firm, and manages several branch locations.

Prior to joining ARS, Cory spent 15 years with two other nationally known financial services firms. He provides a wealth of knowledge and experience in retirement and financial planning.

Cory served in the Air National Guard, where he was named Airman of the Year for the state of Minnesota. His service included several deployments supporting the "War on Drugs" in Panama. His community service includes more than 20 years coaching youth baseball.

Kevin: Cory Davern is with Presidential Wealth Management. Cory, tell us a little about yourself. Where did you grow up?

Cory: I grew up in Superior, Wisconsin, a small town in northern Wisconsin by Lake Superior. I would say I grew up with a blue-collar background, hard-working. Both of my grandfathers were pretty entrepreneurial, and were very impactful people in my life. I also have two younger sisters and both of my parents. I attended a private high school, Duluth Cathedral, which was a college preparatory school. After high school, I attended the University of Minnesota-Duluth for two years. Not knowing what I wanted to do for a career, I fulfilled my military aspirations by joining the Minnesota Air National Guard serving at the 148th Fighter Group in Duluth, Minnesota. After my initial training, I went back to school, and completed my bachelor's degree in English with a coaching minor. I served in the Minnesota Air National Guard for nine years.

I got married in 1996, and then went into the financial service industry in 1997. I started with a company called Primerica Financial Services. I fell in love with helping people plan for retirement, helping them manage their insurance and investment needs. In 1999, I moved to VALIC. Then in April, 2005, I was promoted to a district manager position, which brought me to Colorado. I ran our financial services operations for Colorado and Wyoming. By the time I left VALIC, I had grown my district to 46 advisors. Then I moved to Presidential Brokerage, which became America's Retirement Store, and we recently renamed again to Presidential Wealth Management as a result of new ownership. Same company, we just made a marketing name change in 2014 and again recently in 2017. I was brought in as an executive vice president, so I work on trying to help grow the company, and trying to expand our footprint here in Colorado, and hopefully nationally. I'm an advisor, as well, so I work with clients.

Kevin: So, tell us about your childhood. What was it like?

Cory: I would say pretty normal. I was an active kid. I was involved in sports and a lot of outdoor activities like hunting and camping. I always have been involved in my faith, in church. I went to Catholic school for nine years, and then to a non-denominational religious high school. Close family, Catholic background, Irish Catholic. I met my wife there. I was working at UPS, when I was in college, and met her there.

Kevin: I worked at UPS in college, too. I loaded trucks.

Cory: You did? I unloaded, loaded, and then I did package delivery for a while. When I turned 25 or 26, I reached a point in my life where I said, "Okay, I need to find a real job." I was trying to become an F-16 fighter pilot. That was my goal. I got selected, but I didn't get through the process. I said, "Okay, well I want to be an officer, and I want a full-time career at the base. I'm getting married, planning on having a family, so I need a real job. I can't have four part-time jobs, go to school, and make it work anymore. I need to have a real career."

My enlistment was running out, and nothing happened by then. Maybe I was a bit idealistic at the time. I said, "Well, I need to find something to do." I was going to college to be a teacher. I did my student teaching, and realized I didn't want to be a teacher. But then I found financial services. A friend of mine was in financial services, and thought I'd be really good at it, because I like to educate, to teach and I like to coach. He said, "You'd be great at this." That's how I got started, got licensed, and then worked part-time until I could leave UPS.

Probably the best sales job I did was to get my wife to have enough confidence in me to leave. You know, from a steady paycheck and full benefits to something I'd never done before. So, I moved the family from the nucleus that we knew, to where we didn't really have any family or friends. She had full faith, and we made it work.

Kevin: Were your parents in financial services?

Cory: My dad's an accountant. They had us early, me and then my two younger sisters. He worked on the railroad, and then he did an accounting practice on the side. He was trying to keep my mom home with us for as long as he could. When we were getting close to middle school, she went back to work. She works in the insurance industry as well. My mom's role is a support role for a property and casualty insurance business.

Kevin: What do you know now, that you wish you had known when you started?

Cory: In the financial service industry? I wish I would have known 2008 would have happened before it did.

Kevin: Amen to that.

Cory: I think that would be that you have to be able to market yourself, and you can't let the company do it. You have to do some of that as well, so, don't be afraid to network. But at the same time, as far as knowledge goes, to really spend time learning the planning side of financial services.

When I got started, if you know VALIC, it was okay going to a school, going to a hospital, going to a county, and just getting them to sign up for their retirement plan. Initially there was really no planning, so it was just getting people enrolled. I was basically a glorified enroller for almost two years before I figured out, "Hey, I'm not reaching my full potential, or my clients' full potential, the way I'm doing this. I'm really not addressing the real concerns that they're facing." I had more of a short-term approach—just get them saving.

If I could go back 20 years, I would be holistic from day one. "If you're going to work with me, this is what I require. It's full financial planning. I have to look at everything. I want to review your plan, at a minimum, annually, to make sure nothing has changed negatively and is impacting your short and long term financial security. If something has changed, we want to know the impact that change will have, both in the short and long term, on your financial security to assure we avoid potential crises."

I find that too many people will bury their head in the sand a little bit and think, "Okay, it's not that big of a deal." They don't know what the compounding impact is to a decision—whether it be a decision to stop putting money into investments or savings, or to buy something that is very expensive that they really didn't need and didn't have the means to buy. They don't understand the capital that's now going towards that and how it's impacting their financial security 10, 15, 20 years down the road. We're such an immediate gratification society.

But with my clients who really work with me, and hold me to that standard of meeting with them once a year, we're able to look ahead. We go through every expense. We go through every change. We look at their plan with fresh eyes every time. "Okay, where are the new balances? Did the account values go down? If they went down, why? And what is the impact on your plan? Is there an impact? Is it significant?" What I find is, since I've been doing that, the confidence level of my clients in me, and in their plan, is much higher. It's much better than waiting seven, eight years to look at it again, when you can't undo decisions that were made.

I encourage them, "Whenever you're making a major purchase, say you're going on a trip that costs $1,000 or $2,000, you don't have to bother me with that, just if you're making a significant change." I had a client the other day who had decided to change jobs. I scolded him a little bit, and said, "Okay, why am I finding out now, after you already made the decision? Because if you're changing jobs, do you have the next job in place?" And he didn't. He just got tired of his job. "And so, where is that income going to come from? You and your wife need this income to make all of these other things happen, so how long are we going to be without an income? That jeopardizes a lot that we've been trying to accomplish."

Kevin: That just pushes out the retirement date.

Cory: I don't know how long it will be. And he wants to start his own business. "Okay, great. Have you thought through what that is going to require as far as capital? I'm not discouraging you. If that's your passion, I want you to go after it. But I need to know what the demand on your resources will be, because this change could delay us achieving the planning we've done for your retirement. Your retirement income and protecting your investable assets were goals you told me were so important to you? And, have you and your wife both agreed that you're willing to put that on hold, or sacrifice it, or change that plan in the hopes that this takes off? Because, I can be your optimist, and I can be your pessimist at the same time."

So optimistically, yes, I believe that can work. If you have a good business plan, and you're a great worker. He wants to do some woodworking. So, "If you're great at woodworking and you can find clientele that's going to be buying from you, wonderful."

To be able to make a living at what you love, there's nothing better than that. But I asked him, "Have you thought of the struggle? How are you going to find clients? How are you going to market? What is all that going to take, and what's the time frame before you can actually cash flow this business, so you can actually accelerate this plan that we're on? Have you thought that through?" Unfortunately, his answer was, "No." I told him that that was something we probably should have talked about when he first started having the idea of going into business for himself or changing careers, before he actually did it. That's the importance of planning because we can work around these goals, even if they seem in conflict with each other.

In this example, we have a couple. So, I can go to his wife and ask how she feels about this. If she supports him, I can share how much I can appreciate her being behind him, and supporting his dream, because my wife supported my dream to get into this business. But we always have to be realistic, too. At what cost, at least short term, is that going to be, and are they both willing to pay that price? "I believe with energy and commitment you're going to be able to turn this around, and it will be able to accelerate the plan down the road, but are you willing to make that sacrifice now?"

Sometimes, I find that a person doesn't even know they're doing this. Sometimes that happens, because the communication between couples isn't always good. So, there are times when I'm kind of a marriage counselor. I'll say, "Okay, you guys need to work some stuff out. I'm going to go get some coffee. I'll come back in about 15 minutes. But, you guys need to work this out, because if we're going to battle, we can't accomplish anything. We have to leave the past in the past. Learn from it, but leave it there. Don't bring it back up. Let's focus on where we're going. What do we want to accomplish now, together?"

Kevin: Talk for a minute about ways that you help seniors.

Cory: As a firm, we do a lot of outreach with education to those who are 55 and older. We offer Social Security workshops, health care cost and retirement workshops, and retirement income workshops. Our education events allow people to get a taste of who we are, areas where we can help them, and what it would be like to work with us through all their planning needs. Through planning we can address all their concerns and even those concerns they don't know they have or should have.

Our process is to first understand their financial situation, goals, dreams, fears, and concerns. We start the planning process looking at what our prospective client would like their retirement or financial situation to look like. Once the analysis is done, we can see how realistic their ideas are.

We will spend time analyzing their Social Security options and determine the best time for them to file. We will add in healthcare costs they currently have or should expect to have in retirement. We consider their other living expenses, along with current and future income streams they have, or will need to have, to fund all of the things they want to do throughout their retirement years.

Once we determine the health of their current plan, we work to improve it by addressing all the concerns we find. Once we have a plan that will work for our clients or prospective clients, we can then stress test their plan with things like hyperinflation, unexpected healthcare costs, long-term care events, premature death, higher taxes, etc. We do this to make sure their plan can withstand the challenges they could face somewhere down the road. It's better to have a plan or strategy in place for those unexpected things now versus after they happen.

Once we've completed this planning we work with our clients on things they want us to address. We come up with solutions, add those solutions to the plan to illustrate how the strategy can benefit them, and hopefully implement those strategies.

We can also assess their current investment portfolio. We'll test the risk level of their portfolio to make sure it's aligned with their risk tolerance. You'd be surprised how often it isn't. We can assess the fees in their overall portfolio and help them implement strategies which will reduce their portfolio costs, add more value, or both. In a word, we try to be as "holistic" as possible with the planning we do for our clients and prospective clients. As a result of planning, we can be much more thorough and flexible with how we help our clients achieve their financial goals.

We can also help them more accurately manage their decisions to help provide them the financial security they are seeking. Planning helps our client assess what things can and can't be negotiated. At the end of the planning, often people have to make some decisions. For example, should they retire later? Do they need to re-evaluate the spending and lifestyle they want in retirement? Should they work a little longer, save more, take more investment risk, reposition the portfolio for income and protection, etc.?

For most people, the biggest fear is running out of money, or healthcare costs that they can't plan for and meet, like long-term care. So, let's illustrate a long-term care event. I'll ask, "Do you know what it costs today, per month, for a semi-private room? Let's not even go private for now, just look at a semi-private room. Should you be in a nursing home, or assisted living, or getting 24/seven care at home, or close to 24/seven care at home? What do you think that costs a month?"

They'll throw out a number. And I'll say, "Well, in Colorado, the average is $8,000 a month. That's $96,000 a year. Do you think that cost will go up in the future, or down, or stay the same?" Everyone says up. AARP would say up as well, and they suggest that we use a seven percent inflation rate on anything healthcare related. So, I put that in, $96,000 today, fast forward it 20 years, and now let's say, "Well, this event, the 24/seven care, where it's beyond your spouse, beyond your kids, beyond whoever could help. You need professional care. Say it happens in your mid-80s, that's a $200,000 annual bill. What does that do to your portfolio?"

And if you're married, once whoever has the issue passes away, assuming they pass away in three years, what of your retirement nest egg will be left for your surviving spouse? Is there enough money left for the surviving spouse to live out the rest of their days? Usually not. That's something we probably need to address. "Okay, how do we want to address it?"

You can ignore it and hope it doesn't happen. That is a decision. You could do estate planning and things like that to help mitigate some of it. Then, there's long-term care insurance. There's life insurance with long-term care benefits. There are investment strategies that have income benefits that will increase income for those needs. It's likely a combination of these things working together that will solve the long-term care or health event issue. Also, many people think they have to solve for the whole cost. Often, solving for a portion of it is all one needs to do and still protect their surviving spouse.

Kevin: That's a good point.

Cory: I'll go back and say, "If there's a $200,000 bill in 20 years, how much of it do we have to solve before your surviving spouse doesn't have to worry about their income security?" It's just a number. You just keep plugging the number and increasing it until the red goes away.

We have a very graphical financial planning tool, where if there's a shortfall, the graph will illustrate red, meaning running out of money. Red equals danger, right? Then just start increasing. If you work with me, I'll create a combination of things for you to try to address this at the lowest cost we possibly can. We can't ignore that, now that we know it's there, unless they choose to.

If they don't want to do anything, we'll say, "Okay, this is what we're going to be using your house for." That's where the reverse mortgage comes in. Plan it. Get it set up. Get the line of credit going, and don't touch it. You can't touch it. It's not in that equity build. And maybe after seven, eight, 10 years, if you haven't had to tap it, can you get more equity out of it? Has your house appreciated so much that you could actually get more equity? And is it worth going through the process again to have a bigger line of credit? Better to do it when you have all your faculties than to make a crisis decision.

So, it's planning. That's what we do for seniors, and we try to address all the concerns seniors will be facing. What's the best way to take Social Security? Do you take it now, or do you delay? Do you still have spousal benefits available to you? We look at taxation of their Social Security. We look at what they've saved, look at healthcare costs and what they need to be thinking about there. Then, how it all works together in a plan with the lifestyle they want to lead as well.

We try to help them navigate their decisions on how to go into retirement with as much peace of mind and security as possible. That's always my goal. As I say, "My goal is to help you get to a point where you can retire without worrying." I don't want you worrying about your money. I don't want you to worry if you're protected. If certain events happen, I want you to know that's taken care of so you can go live life. And then, once a year we come back and we check on it, make sure it's okay, more often if you want to. That's my goal, if you choose to work with me. I don't know the situation yet, so there might be some hard decisions that you're going to have to make.

Kevin: What do you like best about what you do?

Cory: There are a couple of things. One, when a couple or an individual comes in, and they're really scared, because they don't think they have saved enough and they can't work anymore. They're at a point emotionally where they just can't see themselves doing it anymore, and they feel trapped. They feel like they have no freedom or choices.

So, they come, and they're usually very timid and sometimes embarrassed. And usually what I hear is, "I've been putting this off a long time because of that fear." Then to be able to calm them, and get them to open up, because it's kind of like going to a financial doctor. They've got to get financially naked with me for me to do my job. You have to be completely honest. Don't hide anything. Otherwise, it's a time bomb that's going to hurt you, and I don't want to hurt you.

So, we go through that. They open up. I get the information, put the plan together, and we find a way to make it work. And often times, those people are the ones who are in the best position, and the plan isn't that hard. It's not that complicated. They've saved enough. They're living frugally. The lifestyle they want to lead in retirement is within their financial ability.

And then the sense of relief. You can actually see them get younger sometimes in front of you when that fear goes away. And then what's really fun is when they come back, and they're still working. And expecting to work for a few more years.

But then I tell them, "Guess what? I ran a version of this with you retiring now, because of what you shared with me about the stress, and what it's doing to your emotional state of being. Work is just this anvil hanging over you, and you can't get out from under it. I wanted to see if there was a way we could accelerate your retirement date forward. So, I ran it with you retiring now." Which isn't what they asked for, but I'll run it. And I say, "You know what? It would take a little bit of work, but we could actually retire you now. How does that make you feel?"

Often times, all of a sudden, they find joy in work again, because they no longer feel trapped. Now they know that they're working because they want to, not because they need to, and that gives them a whole different perspective on not just work, but life.

It's really interesting to see that transformation happen. That's a big highlight. To know you've helped individuals. They're in a better spot now that they've taken your advice. I try and stay in contact with my clients as best I can. I schedule it out, so I don't miss them. I contact them on birthdays and things like that, just to stay in touch.

Some might say, "Well, that's marketing." Well, maybe it is, but I want to stay in touch with them. Often I'll call them out of the blue. They're not expecting it, and I'm catching them just at a point in life where they're making a decision that I should be involved with, and they're not thinking I should be involved with it. It really gives me an opportunity to talk to them. That is a highlight.

Getting to meet their kids, and involving their kids in the planning process. A lot of times parents aren't open to that, but when they are, that's a lot of fun. Because usually their kids are my age, and you make new relationships that way. That's a highlight.

Kevin: Those highlights are all great. So, one of the things we hear from seniors is that they want to stay at home as long as they can, to age in place. And you may have already answered this earlier with another question, but what do you do to help seniors age in place?

Cory: Great question, because you're right, they want to live and die at home. I know that was my grandfather. He passed away four years ago this summer, and his mind was still sound, but his body was failing. I went to visit him in a nursing home. He said he hated it, and told me, "I wish I could just be at home and let this happen there." But it was too hard on my grandma, so he understood why he couldn't. So, I understand firsthand the importance of being in an environment that's comfortable and yours, versus strangers coming in all hours of the night, picking at you, prodding at you, and not really caring. In his words, "I'm just meat on a bed." That's how he felt. At home, at least you feel like your care is better.

So, we do try to help people get there, and stay there. Part of that is helping them understand what it is going to take to be able to stay at home. And the first part is, who they have to help them. I tell them it shouldn't be their spouse, because they're about the same age. So, if you have a man in his 80s who weighs about 200 pounds, and his wife is in her 80s and small, what's going to be her ability to get him out of bed and into and out of the shower? Feeding, dressing, and some of the stuff like that, maybe. But when she has to lift him, do you think she's going to be able to do that?

So, I tell them, "Talk to me about your family dynamic. Do you have kids? Are they a part of your plan?" If the answer is yes, the next question is, "Do they know that?" Because often they don't know, or don't want that. And then I'll ask other important questions. "How well are your kids doing, and do they have their own kids? If your son or daughter has to care for you, it might jeopardize their career, the needs of their own families. Have you considered how caring for you might impact them and do you really want them to provide care for you? You may be asking them to put their life on hold to care for you."

That's the part that parents sometimes forget. We need to understand that we've created a new generation called the sandwich generation, where we have adults taking care of parents, raising kids at home, and they're still in a career. Also, if their kids aren't in a position to help them physically, what about financially? Because if we can't find a solution within their resources for this health event, their children may be in a financial position to help out.

And if a parent needs full-time care, how are they going to manage all of that, and should they? They might want to, and if they can, great. But at some point, when does it go to where it's beyond them, and it needs to go to the next level?

Then I'll just say, "Let's suppose that your health was failing and you wanted to stay at home, but you need care. And let's say that care wasn't available to you within your family or friend network and you had to go to professional services. How are you going to manage your care? What do you have in place now to address this possibility? Are you willing to explore options that could alleviate that concern?" Then maybe it's a collective effort of the family that we put in place. This is a conversation that's not just between the three of us. This is a conversation that needs to happen at the family level.

Kevin: So, what are some of the most common mistakes you see seniors make as they approach, or are in retirement?

Cory: Probably the first one is many have not really put pen to paper on their own, or with someone else, to figure out if they can afford to retire. First thing, as early as possible, I would urge people to start planning. What is it going to take? What do they need to save? What's the number they need saved to finance the rest of their life? Many don't do the hard planning to make sure they've saved enough before they decide to retire.

They go into retirement wondering if they really have enough. If they don't, what can they do make sure they have enough before they put in those retirement papers? Should they work a little bit longer? Save more? Revisit retirement expenses and goals? What are some other choices they have? Work part-time, whatever it might be. If they are determined to retire at a specific age, whether they are financially ready to do so or not, then many have to consider making changes to their retirement vision or risk running out of money before they're done living their retirement.

That's probably the number one thing that I see, that people just haven't really planned well enough. And I understand why, I think, but we have to get over this.

There's a fear factor I believe, to come to someone like me, because it's admitting a weakness, and also because of what's been out in the public. When you have a bad financial advisor or planner, or everyone's thinking, "Wall Street, all they're trying to do is fleece you, and get as much money out of you, and sell you a bunch of products that don't help you, but really help them."

The reality is that's not the majority of our industry. The majority of our industry is hardworking people that really have found a calling to help others with their financial decisions, and they really take care in trying to make good decisions. Different advisors could be working the same problem and come up with different, yet viable and suitable solutions and recommendations. Each advisor has a perspective unique to him or her, but what most of us have in common is a desire to help our clients and put them in a better position than the one they were in before they met us.

The fear of working with an advisor is something we need to get over. Also, we need to start the planning process as early as possible. The people who start earlier are the most prepared. So that's probably mistake number one.

Mistake number two is not really understanding what it's going to cost in retirement. They think, especially if they have a pension, "Okay, well my pension is going to pay me this, and it's close to what I'm already making." But there's no cost of living adjustment, so they don't realize inflation is going to eat away at that pretty soon. They're going to lose purchasing power. When I was at VALIC, we had a lot of people with pension plans who retired, and within three years were asking for their job back. They didn't plan and thought, "Well, I'm going to get $3,000 a month in my pension." They didn't think it was going to be taxed. So, they're not getting $3,000. They're getting $3,000 minus taxes.

Kevin: The senior partner.

Cory: Exactly. IRS. So, they don't think some of those things through. And the reality is they're making a decision to retire and probably haven't spent a lot of time preparing for it. Maybe emotionally they have, but financially, a lot of times, they just haven't. And they're looking, "Social Security will be this much. This will be this much. That's enough." But they don't consider inflation. They don't consider taxes. They don't consider health care costs. It's not their world. It's not their perspective. They don't realize what impact that can have on purchasing power over decades. They're looking at five years. "I've got enough money to get through five years. That means I can retire." And at the end of five years they're saying, "Where do I get income now?"

They don't know how to invest. That's another mistake. When it comes to their investable assets, they don't know how to invest in retirement, because they're still in a growth mode. For 30 or 40 years, they've been in accumulation. It's all about growth. It's not about income.

Well, when you get to retirement, you don't have that job anymore with income that can buy you years if we have a down market or if you make a mistake. When you're in retirement you don't have that luxury to make a mistake. But mistakes are pretty much unavoidable. If you can change your mindset from growth to income and preservation, then with some calculated growth, you take risk out of the portfolio.

Too often I will see people go into retirement with the same amount of risk they had when they were working. They didn't really change their investment strategy for a different phase of life. In one phase of life, you're putting money away. In the next phase, you're taking it out. That requires different strategies.

It's difficult to grow your way through retirement, and you're really subjecting yourself to luck. If I retire today and find myself in a financial year like 2008 my very first year of retirement, I am not recovering from that. If I'm drawing money out every year, there's no way I'm going to recover from that. I'm going to need returns from the market that have never happened before to get back to where I started.

But I could have the same investment platform, and retire a few years before a bad financial year. If you get five or six years of accelerated growth, and then weather a year like 2008, you're in better shape. You just don't know when those returns are going to happen, so it's kind of by luck.

So, we should go into retirement with planning what we need. I like to use a pyramid. The pyramid is, what do I need? What do I have to have? What are my basic expenses? Some people use a financial house. The idea is a foundation. What is the foundation that I need to have in place before I retire, or at least understand as I go into retirement?

First, what are my basic expenses? And what income sources am I going to have that aren't investment related? Social Security, pensions, maybe income off real estate that I've owned for a long time and is going to be consistent. I'll count that in that bottom bucket. Okay, here's the income we know is coming in. Here's the amount of money we need after taxes. Do we have a gap?

If there is a gap we have to address that first, before anything else, because that's what you need just to survive in retirement. So, we look at the portfolio. What do we need to do with the portfolio to fill that gap? And it can't have risk. It can't be taken away by the market. We need to layer in guarantees to make sure the income is there.

Then we look at the threats to that income, such as long-term care events. That's probably the biggest one, and inflation, things like that. That's a harder one to plan for, but you have to try to plan for it somewhat.

Then we look at protection. That's where long-term care can come into play, where life insurance can come into play. If I have a pension, do I have a spousal benefit? Which spousal benefit am I using and why? A lot of times we don't think about it. We say, "But single gives me the most." But if you die, your husband or wife won't get that income. Do they need it? If they need that income, you can't take 100 percent. Let's think it through.

Once that's solved, then I say, "Okay, what makes retirement fun?" That's the quality of life. What are the things you want to do? And what do you want to allocate to that every year? If I can create that through income stream, investments that kick out an income, I never have to touch the principal. In theory, I'll never have to touch the principal; the income will always be there.

Let's say you want $10,000 a year for a trip. Every year you're going to spend $10,000 on a trip. I can create $10,000 of income, and it's there every year, even if the value of an investment is going up and down. So, with the income you can still do things in life. If it's down, you don't have to touch the principal. If the income is suffering because of it, we can change the plans.

Then, denial. I think the third one is probably denial. Denying and saying, "A healthcare event happens to other people, not me. Premature death happens to other people, not me." That denial, and not planning for some of those. They're not the fun part of planning. They're not the fun part of conversations, but those are the things that can damage someone's income security. And to really be open to that, if they can. It's usually men that struggle the most, because I think we have to show that we're strong.

Kevin: Bulletproof.

Cory: "Nothing's going to happen to me, and I'm in control of everything." The reality is that there's so much we're not in control of, and if we could just let go of that. I think women do a better job of seeking advice and acting on it. I know that's kind of stereotypical. I don't mean it to be that way, but that's what my experience has been. It's harder to convince men to do some of the protection stuff, because they think they're invincible.

Women don't have that, because I think women seek security, in general, more than men do. Men seem to typically be the thrill seeker, the adventurer. We'll take the risk. And women are actually better planners. Women do a better job planning for retirement on the whole, than men do. They do a better job of managing risk overall than men do.

I know that with my own wife. My wife has taught me to pull back a little bit on the reigns, because I'm a thrill seeker. Not with my clients' money. I'm actually probably ultra conservative with their money. I like a little bit of adventure in things. I always have to balance that. But those are the key mistakes people make.

And, in general, I feel most people really don't understand what it takes to plan for what will likely be a third of your life in retirement. If you retire at 60 and you live to 90, you'll have spent a third of your life in retirement.

Kevin: Especially nowadays. Is there a product or technique or a service that you offer, that you wish more of your senior clients knew about?

Cory: Because we focus so much on planning, I never put a strategy or product in front of the plan. The plan dictates what we do. So, I think I would come back to planning on that, and let the needs, desires, goals, and objectives of the couple or the individual I'm working with dictate the product or strategy they should look at using. They need to be more open to things that are income heavy, with guarantees. We get Suze Orman and some of these people that are against certain strategies, but they're not on the hook when their strategy doesn't work.

So, I would say look at things that are more income driven. Don't be afraid to explore things that are designed to protect you, even in the growth portion of your portfolio. I think it makes sense to manage risk as much as possible in retirement.

I talked earlier about the financial pyramid. That third part of the pyramid would be more legacy planning, or your inflation hedge. That's your growth piece. Whatever's not needed in those other layers can go into that top piece and be more traditionally invested for growth. But even with that, you might want to be mindful of trying to minimize risk to when markets turn over. There are lots of different strategies to do that.

Kevin: At the end of the day, people want cash flow in retirement, right? That's the bottom line.

Cory: Yes, but to me, not a lot of people focus on that, and they're trying to grow their way through retirement. So, if I'm spending five, I've got to earn five. If I want to spend eight, I have to earn eight. The risk there is that you earn the eight, so you spend the eight, now you're used to that type of spending. Next year you're down 10, but you want to spend eight, so now you're down 18. To get back to even, you've got to make 22 or 23 percent on your money the following year, without a distribution. Right now, I'm taking a bigger distribution out. Now eight is like 12, so I've got to earn another 22 on top of that. Because I'm taking out 12, I've got to have almost a 30 percent rate of return or more, just to get back to even. That's putting a lot of hope in the market always being there for you.

For the money that I don't need for income, fine, let that be growth oriented. If a client is telling me the lifestyle they want, I'm trying to create the income that they need for that. My goal is to do that with as little impact to principal as possible. It's hard to avoid it 100 percent, but I try to minimize that as much as possible.

Kevin: Tell me about a recent senior client you helped. Not

naming any names, of course. But what was their situation? What were they hoping to accomplish? How did you help them?

Cory: The one that's coming to mind was a situation where I didn't know if I would be able to help, to be honest. She didn't have a lot of savings, maybe $100,000. She's 63 or 64 years old and wanted to retire in the next four years. The good news is, she had no debt. The house was paid off. No car debt. No credit card debt. So, she was doing a very good job of living within her means. But I was fearful of the lifestyle that she wants to lead. She didn't want to, in her mind, "lose the house to a reverse mortgage," so that's off the table, because that is the legacy to her kids.

Because she's done such a good job at minimizing expenses and living within her means, we actually can make it work. There were some challenges, but we were able to find a way to make that work. As a result, she's going to have income security probably into her early 90s without much invested, and that's no market risk. She wanted nothing allocated to the market. So, she has no market risk. It's all income based. I told her, "If you get to this point, and if life hasn't thrown you any curve balls, then you're going to have to use that house." But she knows that going in, and she was very appreciative of the fact that we shared that with her.

So that was a situation that looked pretty dire. I didn't know if we would be able to make it happen, but it's done, again, through the planning. And people don't understand how many hours can go into that. Throwing strategies and strategies, at a problem, until you find something that can work.

Kevin: So, Cory, who's an ideal client for you?

Cory: The ideal client, the one that allows us to do the full gambit of what we offer as a firm, or as individual advisors, would be somebody who is probably in their 50s or older. They have savings. They've invested. They have retirement goals. They're actively working towards those goals—maybe not the most efficient way, but they are working. They want advice. They want a relationship with somebody, and it doesn't mean they have to take the advice. I encourage my clients, "If you disagree, please disagree. I like debate. Sometimes I learn from your experience, or your fear, or what you see as an opportunity. I can learn from that."

I'm not locked into one way of thinking for everybody. I want to build a plan around what you want, what you need. So sometimes we have debates. I like that because that allows me to learn who you really are. I know where the lines are being drawn. Someone that has some opinions, but is open to change as well, and we work together. It's not me dictating, and it's not them just following. It is a partnership. It's give and take. And understanding that everything is being done with their best interest in mind. So, whatever I recommend, it's because I believe it works. I'm going to show you how it works. If it can't improve your plan, I'm not going to show it to you. The client may disagree with a recommendation and I want them to share it with me. Let's be open about it. It doesn't mean we can't work together. It just means we have to work around this.

As for an investment dollar amount, what I find is, if someone is at retirement with $250,000, we can help, but it's going to be difficult. There are going to be some potential pitfalls in the future that we're going to have to address. Depending on what type of income sources you have, you probably need $500,000 or more. And again, it depends. Do you have pensions? What's your Social

	Security? What's your lifestyle like? But the ideal client would probably be in that group.
Kevin:	And what would be the first step that you would want them to take?
Cory:	The first step would be to come in and see us. We offer a discovery session. That's kind of what you and I are doing now. We're learning about each other. No pressure, you don't have to write a check. You can come in. We can sit down. We can talk about your major concerns. We can introduce you to a couple tools that we use to help solve it. But what we're trying to do is find out, "Can I help you? Are we a good fit?"

And I know I'm being interviewed as well, and they're doing the same thing. But after the end of that conversation, if they feel that it's worth pursuing, then we go to the next phase. It starts the client process, where they need to share all their financial information. They're not going to hold anything back. So, that's what the discovery session is. It gets them into the planning process.

And then what it means to them at the end is they're going to have all their questions answered. They're going to have a strategy. They're going to know how it's going to look, how it's going to work, when income is going to turn on and where it's going to come from. They're going to find out whether they have any reason to be concerned in the future. And if there is a concern in the future, then we're going to work together to address it, and try to minimize that as much as possible.

But now, they can walk away from that knowing they have someone they can call on at any time, and they can live their retirement the way they want to. They told us what they wanted from it, and we created it. And if there are some challenges, we're going to talk to them about that. And say, "Okay, we probably can't do this, but we could do this instead. Is that a good compromise?"

Kevin: How do your ideal clients find you?

Cory: We've done a lot of marketing on radio. We do educational workshops pretty much every month on various topics—Social Security, Medicare, retirement income, tax planning, and estate planning. Those are just some of them. We do direct mail. We do direct mail marketing whenever we have events. One of the things that I think we need to do a better job of is referral within our own client base. And helping our clients be advocates of ours to introduce us to the people they care about, who probably need our services as well. Or maybe they've had a bad experience with one of the professionals in our industry. If they're open to giving someone a chance to restore their faith in our community, and they might come in that way.

Kevin: What's the biggest challenge you're facing right now?

Cory: I think it's the same for every advisor. Getting in front of other people. All the surveys that are done by independent organizations come back and say the same thing. People aren't prepared for retirement. They're not prepared for a healthcare event. They don't understand their Social Security. They don't understand their Medicare. They're making mistakes. They're overpaying. So, there's all this information that comes out that tells us how much we're needed. Yet, it's hard to get people to come and get the help that we offer. Also, for most people, their investment performance is way below what indexes are doing. The S&P 500 average is eight to nine percent over a 10-year period, yet the average investor earns two to three percent and it never changes. Things like that.

Those are the big challenges. The biggest challenge is to help people get over these hurdles.

We had a meeting the other day, and asked, "As a company, how can we be more attractive to prospective clients? How can we dismantle the barrier between us and those who could benefit from our help? How do we get over the hurdle, so people are inclined to come in and not see us as a threat and are not anxious.

I think there's this general fear of our industry. I think there are a lot of different fears that we deal with. But there's something that's holding people back, and part of it is trust. Part of it is just trust in the industry, trust in financial professionals. I hear it a lot.

In fact, I heard this from a client the other day. Now, it took me a year and a half to get them to be a client. They finally did. And the husband said, "You know, Cory, I want to pay you a compliment. We've been with several advisors, but you're the first that actually listened, heard, and then implemented a strategy, or helped us implement a strategy, that was focused on what we desired, what we wanted. And then you were open about what the fees were, how you were going to be compensated. So, we knew exactly what we were getting into when we got into it. No one's ever done that. They always try to steer me into something that they wanted, not what I wanted." Then he added, "It doesn't hurt us that it's working really well right now." That's an example.

They had come to a Social Security workshop, and they just wanted an answer on Social Security. They really weren't interested in pursuing a relationship with me. But I just kept talking to them. I just would touch base with them. "Hey, I know you have this fear. Have you found a solution? How is it working? Can I be of help? Will you come in and just let me do the planning? I won't charge you for it, just so you can get a feel for what it is I do. It might restore some confidence." It was a process for them.

Kevin: What's the best advice you've ever received?

Cory: There's been a lot of it. When it comes to this industry, one stands out. I take things personally, too personally sometimes. So, when you put a lot of time into somebody, and they decide not to work with you, that hurts. I'm not going to sugar coat it. It hurts. I look at everything I did. "Okay, what did I do? What did I say? How did I position? Did I do anything to push them off? What could I have done better?" And someone said to me, "You know, you can't beat yourself up, because you're successful for whatever reason. You have clients that are saying yes. Not everyone is going to say yes. Focus on the next yes." You can't take it personally. That's probably some of the best advice.

Kevin: Anything you'd like to share that I haven't asked you already?

Cory: I may already have said this, but I think I'll come back to it. Don't view what we do based on people who've made the news in the wrong way. We all know and watch the news; it's all negative. It's so refreshing when they do a feel-good piece, because you would think that the world is going to hell in a hand basket if you just watched the news. You can't help but think, "What's this world coming to? How are we going to ever survive? Everyone's out to kill everybody." You just walk away. You become depressed. And wonder why you would want to leave your front door. It's very easy to go down that path.

I try to remind people that the majority of people that have chosen or have answered the call to be in this industry, view it as a service. We want to help. We're not trying to take advantage of people. There are some that do, unfortunately, but the majority of us in this industry are not. We're here to do the right thing. We really are.

Kevin: Where can our audience go to learn more about you?

Cory: Our website, http://www.americasretirementstore.com/ would be a good place to start. Come to any of our events. We have offices in Colorado Springs, here in Greenwood Village, and in Loveland. Pretty much every month we'll have something going on at those three locations. We'll even do some community outreach, where we'll go into other communities. We'll do a rec center, a library, a restaurant, a hotel, a conference room-type thing, like Lakewood, Wheat Ridge, for example. They may not want to drive down to Greenwood Village. So, on occasion we'll run events up there, so we can get closer to them. It's all on the website. Or they can call us at 303-694-1600.

Kevin: Awesome. Thank you so much, Cory.

CHAPTER 14

Carolyn Brent

Carolyn A. Brent is an award-winning and bestselling American author and eldercare legislation advocate. Designated as an Editor's Choice, she was reviewed by the Library Journal as well. Verdict: excellent!

Brent is also known as a bodybuilder and Health & Wellness Guru. She is the founder of Across All Ages and two nonprofit organizations, CareGiverStory Inc. and Grandpa's Dream. Visit: CareGiverStory.com

---

Kevin: Carolyn, tell us where you are from.

Carolyn: I was born in Oklahoma City. I spent my childhood years in Denver, Colorado, and at the age of 18 I went to Boulder, Colorado, for school. After that, I ended up moving to beautiful southern California. I moved to Los Angeles and Seattle, Washington. I've kind of been all over the place. But, now, at the age of 60, I made a decision to live in warmer climates. So, I live in Del Ray Beach, Fla., and I absolutely love it here.

Kevin: It sounds like you've lived in some beautiful places.

Carolyn: Yes, I have. I feel very blessed to have been able to travel and that was a form of education. I'm just very, very grateful.

Kevin: That's great. Before we started, you mentioned how you've lived in Colorado and now you're a beach person. I, myself, am from Southern California, so I am a beach person, too.

Carolyn: I love it. I love the beach. I get my energy from the ocean and I get a lot of creative ideas when I'm walking on the beach. My father's spirit gives me a lot of wonderful things to write about. That's where I get all this brilliant information—just walking along the beach, thinking and meditating.

Kevin: What kind of work did your parents do?

Carolyn: My mother was a homemaker, as well as a nurse, when she did work. My father sold land. He was a land developer and then he ended up becoming a minister in his later years in life. I think at the age of 55, he went back to school, got his doctoral degree in theology, and became a full-time minister.

Kevin: I know you're quite accomplished with different things you've done, especially in the area of elder care. Tell us a little bit about how you got drawn into that and a little bit more about the calling, or mission, that you're pursuing with your life and career.

Carolyn: My life's mission is becoming a caregiver legislative advocate for elders and caregivers. It wasn't something where I said, "When I grow up that's what I want to do." I worked full time in pharmaceuticals and loved what I was doing. I was a clinical education manager and I saw myself retiring in that career. But, unfortunately for me, when I was 12, my parents divorced. My mother went her separate way, and both my parents remarried. In their later years in life, my father developed dementia.

I became my father's full-time caregiver. I didn't even know I was a caregiver. I went to Lamar, Colorado, to visit him, because dad wasn't answering his telephone. When I saw my father, he had lost 30 pounds. They had taken him to the VA. The doctor said, "Thank God you are your father's caregiver, because his hemoglobin is down and he could have died." I said, "No. I'm not his caregiver, I'm his daughter." That was the time in which I became his caregiver. That was back in 1997, and that was the first time I had even heard the words, "You are a caregiver." We never want our parents to get sick. We think they're going to live forever. We know they're going to pass away, but the hope is they are healthy and live forever. But, that was not the case when it came to my dad.

When I started taking care of my father, I still maintained my career in the pharmaceutical industry. At the time, I had eight adult siblings living around the country and I was the only one that was not married. I did not have children. They said, "Carolyn, you take care of dad. You do the job." And twelve years later, my dad had a massive hematoma, which is bleeding on the brain. My family thought dad was dying. I found myself in three different courts with fictitious litigation. That simply means the person is using the law to press charges without cause, which is evil work for money. Unfortunately for me, that turned me into an advocate, because I thought, "How can someone use the court system in order to become a caregiver for someone that they've never facilitated care for in 12 years?"

The last time I went to court, I shared with the judge that the laws need to be changed. When I walked out of court I said, "I'm going to work to change the laws so that the loved ones can put their legal documents in place legally and know that it's done correctly. They will know that the caregivers will actually be protected on the back end of caregiving when they're a law-abiding caregiver." The profession found me, I did not sign up. It's just something that happened. That's how I found out that was my passion. I couldn't let it go.

I've been advocating by using legislature. I ended up writing three books on the subject. Regarding two of the books, one is in the Library of Congress and the other one is in universities as a learning module. I was blessed for it to be in there. But, no one had ever written on preparing for end of life medically, financially and emotionally—and how to care for yourself. I was the first person to write that. I feel honored, and I want to help caregivers. It doesn't matter from which caregiving walk of life they are.

A loved one doesn't necessarily need to be old for caregiving to start. It could be anyone that's having a little bit of difficulty. It could be a medical issue that starts out very, very slowly and then it titrates up. I've turned into an advocate. I never knew that that's what I was. Wikipedia would have me as a person that is noble and they call me a "legislation advocate." That's what they named me. And I figured, okay, that's what I am, because that's what I do.

I feel very blessed, honored, and happy to be in this industry. I cannot even see my life without the advocacy work that I'm doing. When I help others, it's really helping me, because I could have gotten depressed from it. There are over 65 million unpaid caregivers caring for a family member or a loved one, and they're paying and contributing over half a trillion dollars a year in unpaid caregiving services. People don't know that there are family caregivers taking care of mom, dad, and children. They're using their own resources. I really want the American population to know that we are all a caregiver in some kind of way. Get your legal end-of-life documents in place if you're over the age of 21, because that will cover all 50 states. Have these documents done, because you don't necessarily have to be old in order to prepare for end of life. I advise families to have end-of-life conversations and for everyone to know what their end-of-life wishes are. Turn it into a family affair.

Kevin: That's tremendous. Carolyn, as you go through your day, and your career, speaking and writing books and talking to legislators, what are some highlights that really motivate you or are satisfying to you?

Carolyn: I love that question. What has motivated me was when I was a caregiver for my dad and working full time, I totally forgot about myself. I worked with a broken foot, which threw my back out of whack. I still deal with long-term pain that I will have for the rest of my life, because I said, "I've got to go to work. I've got to get that big paycheck and take care of dad." I had him in private assisted living when I needed someone to watch over him. Even if you have a job that you love, you've got to learn how to take care of yourself. The number one thing that I learned was how to take care of myself emotionally, financially, legally and physically.

Last year, at the age of 60, I went upstate in Florida and won a national figure bodybuilding competition. The reason why I did it was because I'm writing about health. I wanted to try to get myself in the best possible health I could be in to really try to prevent some of the challenges that I was born with, like hypertension. It runs in the family. My mother died at 63, my brother died at 53, my sister died two years ago at 49, all from myocardial infarction, which is a heart attack. I said, "What can I do to live a richer life so I can live longer? What can I feed my body that is going to help me grow older gracefully, and so that I can embrace it?" That's what I learned from that whole situation.

I brought in the medical know how, because I have that background in pharmaceuticals. That was one of the most educational job experiences I've ever had, because I dealt with regular MDs and the doctors behind the microscope, who were looking for new and improved organisms to make the chemical drugs. There are products and compounds that we absolutely need that are going to help us. I always try to share with folks that if they could use herbals or anything holistic as their first line of treatment and then go to something stronger like a medication if they have to, we can control a lot of the diseases. I have hypertension and I have high cholesterol, but it's controlled through diet and exercise, as well as the way I think, what I eat, and the people with whom I associate. It's totally amazing. Yes, all of the photos that people see of me, they're real life, real-time photos. I feel so blessed because I don't know what 60 looks like, and I wear 60 very well.

Kevin: When we help people with reverse mortgages, we know they want to stay in their home as long as possible and not go to a facility until they have to. What advice do you give clients as you meet with them to help them stay in their home as long as possible, to age in place?

Carolyn: I highly recommend that a family gets together to have that crucial conversation about finances and mortgage. I believe in reverse mortgage. I believe someone who is 80 years old and still healthy and who is still making a mortgage payment, should be able to age in place. My brain doesn't calculate those figures, but there are a lot of folks out there who don't even know about reverse mortgage. I've asked. Once again, I don't understand why an 80-year-old or 70-year-old or 65-year-old is not thinking in terms of, "What can I do to have better quality of life? How can I just pay for my taxes at the end of the year and live a life of abundance and fullness now?" I love what you do. That's the way I share it with people.

A lot often people ask me, "Carolyn, what about my family? We want to keep it in the family and we don't want X, Y, and Z." I say you have to do your homework and sign the right reverse mortgage. I also say if your loved one gets sick, heaven forbid, if they have a home, guess what? They've got to cash it out before they can get on Medicaid, something that is going to help them. They'll cash it out and then they don't have anything. When they're healthy and enjoying themselves, your loved one will always feel more comfortable for as long as he or she can be around their familiar surroundings, which is the home that they've purchased and built for themselves.

Kevin: When you work with clients, what are some of the most common mistakes you see your clients making when they're trying to plan to stay in their home?

Carolyn: The number one mistake is when they've never put any legal documents in place and are lacking knowledge about everything. Once again, this is a true story. An 80-year-old was making health payments and I said, "Why are you making health payments?" He said, "I've been in my home for X number of years, and I'm in good condition, good shape." I asked him, "Why don't you put your home in reverse mortgage?" He didn't know that reverse mortgage existed. I'm thinking he must not watch television; something's wrong with this picture. I always share with people, either on radio, television or through my writing, to do your homework. Take responsibility, think about where you want to be when you're 60. Reverse mortgage, does it start at 65, Kevin?

Kevin: 62.

Carolyn: Okay, 62. I'm 60 years old. In two more years, you bet your bottom dollar I'm going to do a reverse mortgage. Why? Because it makes sense. It doesn't make sense for me to be making mortgage payments when I could write more books, travel, and just do the things that I enjoy doing because life is so precious and it's so short. To me, it's a part of proper planning.

Once again, when it comes to reverse mortgage, I believe that a person should do their homework. Check out several companies. Feel comfortable with the agent that is representing you. I love the fact that you're writing a book and you're doing your homework, because I've got to tell you, over 55 percent of the US population does not have any end-of-life wishes in place. That simply tells me they may not have a reverse mortgage, because it seems to me that would go hand in hand with what your final wishes are. Wouldn't you agree with that?

Kevin: I really do. What we find is it's an education thing. We need to help make sure people understand what their options are. When they do, they just realize they don't have to live in poverty in their golden years.

Carolyn: Absolutely. I'm a firm believer that we should start living our lives right now, especially when you're 62 years old and especially when you're retired. A mortgage to me, it's in buckets; it's like being in a financial prison as far as I'm concerned. When you can let go of that financial prison you have freedom to take flight. You can fly around if you want to fly, if you want to travel. Whatever your hobbies are and the things you've always wanted to do, then you can do it. It's freeing. I think it will help a person to actually stay healthier longer, because a lot of folks are worried about their finances. They're still trying to do that hustle and they're not enjoying life. That is a reverse mortgage. I'm definitely a proponent for a reverse mortgage.

As a matter of fact, I want to put your business on my website, and you'll be the go-to person for a reverse mortgage. I actually started a column on my website for reverse mortgage. That's how much I believe in it. The only reason I'm doing it is because people don't understand how it works. Or maybe they've heard some horror stories from a relative that doesn't know how it works. They're walking around in fear thinking, "Oh no, the banks are going to take away my home from me." That's not the case. When you get the documents, read them. They can get it embedded by an attorney to substantiate whatever it is they're getting ready to sign. I just find that knowledge is power, and I try my best.

I love writing; it forces me to do research. I'm going, "Wow, look at all these nuggets I'm getting." That's why I'm happy, I'm healthy and I'm trying to live a life of financial freedom, period. When I'm dead and go home to be with God, then my son can say, "Mom lived her life fully, because she really enjoyed herself." But, I'm not going anyplace. I'm having way too much fun.

Kevin: That's great. You've been at this for a while now. What do you know now that you wish you had known when you started?

Carolyn: Everything I write about is what I wish I had known. I wish I had known about the financial woes of growing older and getting sick. I wish I had known what it means to have the right insurances and right safeguards in place. I wish I would have known about protecting myself as a caregiver on the back end of caregiving, just in case the families disagree with someone's wishes. The list of what I've wished for goes on and on. That is why I've written the three books on the subject matter. It's so important.

A person nowadays doesn't have any reason to be like I was. I was looking for information and I couldn't find it. I was looking for information on adult sibling rivalry. I couldn't find it. I searched high and low and then finally I ended up stumbling across a website by the name of Carolyn Rosenblack. She's an elder law attorney. I asked to interview her and she said yes. I interviewed her and she shared with me information about adult sibling rivalry, what to do with it, and how to avoid it. That made me wonder, why isn't this in a book? Then I learned about fictitious litigation. I had never even heard of that until I did a national testimony in front of the California State Legislatures. They coined it as "fictitious litigation." That is when I realized I'm going to have to do something about this.

I started writing. Once again now, my work is in the Library of Congress in Washington, D.C. CBS and ABC gave me my own show for 14 months to go through the whole book, because they found this is information the public needs to know. Now, I'm working strictly on how to combine preparing for end of life and enjoying the journey of life to your golden years. That's the project I've been working on for five years. I talk about the importance of self-care. It's so important. Sometimes we get so wrapped up in our jobs, careers, raising children, and spending time with family and friends, that we forget about ourselves. We forget ourselves even from a financial standpoint. Many 62 year olds are still working full-time jobs and they're still making mortgage payments. They don't even realize they can take some of that pressure off of themselves and perhaps retire at 65 instead of waiting until they're 80 or 90, because they want to pay off their mortgage.

It makes more sense to enjoy your life while you're here on this earth. Do it and do it well without having the financial stress that keeps people stressed out and causes diseases and so many other health issues, because of not properly planning.

Kevin: You're preaching to the choir here. That's very well said.

Carolyn: Thank you. I believe so strongly in what I say and so I write about it. I practice what I talk about. I have to tell you, it's helped me. Being a writer, being an author, being an advocate, draws me to research. I love doing research and I find a wealth of knowledge. That's something no one can take from you. I always share with people that the knowledge is out there, really in this one little book. If you care to read it, there's a wealth of knowledge from doctors and lawyers about real estate. I interview real estate reverse mortgage folks on my show, because I believe in it. It just makes so much sense, it really does.

It keeps your loved one independent longer. The longer they're independent, perhaps, the healthier they're going to be. They're not going to be depressed, they're not going to be displaced, they're not going to feel that they're a burden on anyone or worry about the family deciding to sell their home and put them in a senior living environment. I wrote a book about that, too, a chapter on that.

I went very, very, very deep in that. That's when cost becomes totally out of whack, because that industry is not regulated. In the case example, I started out at $2,000 a month for my dad. By the time it was over, I was paying $6,500 cash. I'm not talking about getting any public assistance, just cash out of pocket for my father. The bottom line is this: when people are prepared early and they have a plan, the family can really see that vision and then things make sense. I believe our loved ones should stay independent for as long as they possibly can. If they have a home, don't look at that as your inheritance. Look at giving your parents, or giving your loved one the best possible life they can live right now, as long as they're healthy.

Kevin: Carolyn, it's so refreshing to talk to someone like you who is passionate and informed and really has a "client first" mentality. What are some of the things that you really enjoy about what you do? You write, speak, travel, and interact with lawmakers. Give me a few highlights of what really gets you up, energized, and going in the morning.

Carolyn: It's really simple. When someone writes me a personal message and tells me how I have impacted their life with either the words that I say, what they have read, or have seen that I'm doing—that gives me chills. I know somebody's listening. It's something just that small that motivates me, because my mission is to help people.

Something really just blew my mind, while I was driving home from a visit with the IRS. You know that was not a pretty visit when the IRS wants to audit you and you're with the auditor for hours. I was wondering, "What did I do to deserve this from the IRS?" Although it turned out to be successful, I was still scared out of my mind. Because it's not often a person gets a special invitation from the IRS. But, I'll never forget September 9. I was driving from Central Florida back down to South Florida, which is like 175 miles. I was going, "I'm glad this is over with." Then I got phone call from my publicist. She said, "Carolyn, you need to pull over and read your email." I pulled over to read my email and it said that Thorndike Books, which is a learning center (they're huge), now has your book in universities and colleges and libraries in large print, throughout the country.

I don't even know how that all took place. But when a person says, "Thank you, Carolyn," or even being on your show, when you said, "Carolyn, I'd really like to interview you." I'm going "Wow, how did they find me?" I still have a very humble heart, because I'm doing what I believe my life's mission is. That's what gets me up.

I keep telling myself I can't die until the laws are changed. I feel like it's been 10 years that I've been knocking at the doors and it's still not happening. But you know what? I believe it's going to happen one day. I believe that many millions of Americans will know about the law I'm trying to pass for fictitious litigation. I'm going to break it down in layman's terms so people can understand. When a subsidiary, a person that has never been in your life, takes you from one court to the next and to the next, just to cause you harm, even though it's not even a valid suit, they're just trying to wreak havoc in your life. That's called a fictitious litigate.

Right now, across the U.S., that's considered a misdemeanor. The judges slap the person on their hand and say, "Don't do it again. We're going to fine you $1,000." But when a person is being dragged through different jurisdictions and court for things that are not true, it really, really takes a mental, financial, and legal toll on that person that's being wrongfully accused of something. I've been trying to get that turned into a felony in order to stop a person from practicing that. That's where my passion comes in for litigation.

I just want families to have a happier ending than what my family had. If I could just move one person, whether it's through an email, getting a book deal that I had no idea was going down, or even being offered to be on a radio show or television, it tells me that what I've been called to do is impacting people. Whether it is one person at a time or millions at a time, I don't know which one it does, but that keeps me going.

Kevin: As people find you and you have all these opportunities, talk for a minute about what an ideal client is for you. Who is the person that you're trying to help the most?

Carolyn: I personally do not deal with one-on-one. I want to make it really clear, because people ask me, "Can you consult with me?" I always have to gratefully say, "No, but I can refer you." The reason why I don't do one-on-one, as far as clients, is because it's very emotional when a person is talking about end-of-life and family issues. That kind of brings me into their family drama. In order for me to keep a drama-free life for myself, I do television, radio and platform presentations, only because that's my area of expertise.

But I always will refer out. That's why I want to put, with your permission of course, your information on my website. I'm sure there are thousands of people in Colorado, who after they hear the radio show, are going to want to find out more about you. I'm a great resource referral person. I call my website a resource portal, because I talk about anything from real estate, to death and dying, to beauty. You name it; it's all there. I refer attorneys on a national level. I love it, because I find that I want to take the work off of people. I don't want a person to feel like they have to do their own research, when I've done it all, and I've vetted people, and I believe in certain things. It's there for them to have if they want it.

I even have a book club with many different books, including caregiving books. A person may not need what I have, but there's something perhaps on there that they want, and it's just taking them like to Amazon or Barnes & Noble. It's a research portal, so that's how I deal with clients. I refer them out.

Kevin: What's the biggest challenge that you're facing right now? You mentioned 10 years of trying to get the legislature changed. Is that the biggest challenge or is there something else?

Carolyn: There are two things. I don't consider them challenges anymore. I consider them areas of opportunity. I switched the word from "challenge" to "opportunity," because, had it not been for those 10 years, I would not have seven books. You know that in the early years, I was angry. I wanted to make a difference overnight; nobody knew who I was. But over time, it really, really humbled my heart. It really helped me to talk to over 1,500 caregivers to see what the problems were that they faced in their personal caregiving experience. This culminated in the book, *The Caregiver's Companion: Caring for a Loved One Medically, Financially and Emotionally While Caring for Yourself.*

Over time, the challenges have turned into areas of opportunity for me, because the legislators know I'm not going anyplace. I was actually speaking in February in California. There's a really great lobbyist group that asked me to speak with them. Now I have 30 lobbyists that are like the soldiers out trying to do this for all of us. It's been a long process, but through the negativity came positive opportunity.

In regard to wellness, I have bone-on-bone in my spine. I have challenges with my health, on which I work on a daily basis, that keep me motivated to try to stay healthy. But, now that's turned into the creation of a wellness center. The wellness center that I will be creating is for people. I don't care if they are caregivers or if they've worked in banking for 30 years. Anyone who is tired of being sick, and tired of being sick and tired, the wellness center is there to help jumpstart a person's health. It will teach them how to eat again, to learn how to manage their health, to learn how to turn challenges and situations into areas of opportunity. That is really the way we look at it.

I had to change the way I was thinking. It all started on someone else's radio show 10 years ago. She said, right on the air, "Carolyn, you sound angry. Can I talk to you after the show?" I said, "Yes." She helped to change my life. I turned that angry person into a passionate person, because I understood I was angry. There are a lot of characteristics of an angry person, because of maybe things that have happened to them. I always share with caregivers it's okay to be angry. Once we get that anger out, then we go to the acceptance part, and the grieving and, all the different layers of Kubler Ross, the five areas of grieving. Once you understand why you're angry, we can get back to what we need to do to reach acceptance. We can focus on how we can turn that anger into something positive that's going to make a difference in your personal life and for others.

Kevin: That's beautiful. I love changing it from challenge to opportunity. That's a great way to think about it.

Carolyn: I look at life like that. Once again, the IRS called me up and I'm thinking, "Oh, no." The opportunity for me was, now I learned a lot from the IRS. I asked questions and they answered me. I never knew I could write off X, Y, and Z. It was a favorable meeting. But, I was really scared at first. Because, you see these commercials that scare you to death, that say, "Call us, don't go and feed the big, bad wolf IRS by yourself." I said "Oh, no. I'm an advocate." If I'm an advocate then I knew I had done nothing wrong. I said, "If I'm an advocate for others, let me be an advocate for myself." If there's something that was done wrong on my taxes, then it will be corrected. That's exactly what happened. It was a scary, but beautiful experience. It really was.

Kevin: What's the best advice that you've ever gotten?

Carolyn: The best advice that I've ever gotten came from my father. He always told me, "Carolyn, you never give up."

As a matter of fact, I have a letter that he wrote me that's in my office on my wall, that I always read when I'm like, "Why am I doing this, why?" I read that letter and dad said that challenges and stumbling blocks will come in your life. They are to be expected. But, it's how you deal with the tragedies, and how you work at them. You've got to look at it a little bit differently. Whatever you do, you cannot give up.

I'm going to give you a perfect example. One of my doctors, about eight years ago, said, "Carolyn, if you're 18 pounds heavier, you're going to be in a wheelchair, because you're bone-on-bone in your spine. Your bones won't be able to support the weight." I said, "Oh no, I'm not going to be in a wheelchair." I could have gotten depressed that day, and started eating bonbons and cookies and candy. I started thinking, "What can I do to help myself, to turn my body into a machine of wellness?" I refused to believe I'm going to ever be in a wheelchair. I had to change the way I was thinking. This was an opportunity for me to check out what I'm putting in myself, so I don't have these inflammation issues. I still get inflamed, and that's just from wear and tear and having pain, but I know what will cause it. I know if I eat, let's say, a hot dog, I'm going to be in trouble the next day. It's going to cause havoc on my body. I'm using that as an example. Why would I eat something that's going to make me sick? I started eliminating things from my diet in order to feel better.

Going back to your original question, the best advice I was ever given was never to give up. I don't give up on getting the laws changed. I will not give up on my own health, which is going to help me help other people who are having challenges with their own personal health. I will not give up on living a debt-free life. I won't give up until those folks out there know reverse mortgage is the way to go when you're 62 years old. It is the way to get financial freedom unless they're able to pay their home off in full.

Kevin: This has been so delightful to get to know you and learn more about what you do and how you help people. If people wanted to read some of your books, what are the titles?

Carolyn: Everything that I do—including videos or the CBS and ABC channels where they can see interaction with myself and an anchor, all the different subjects that we talked about today—is there for their knowledge.

The title of the first book is called *Why Wait? The Babyboomer's Guide to Preparing Emotionally, Financially and Legally for a Parent Death*. That was published back in 2011. One of the two books that are in the Library of Congress, and also in libraries across the country, is called *The Caregiver's Companion: Caring for Your Loved One Medically, Financially and Emotionally While Caring for Yourself*.

I also have three books on my website. One is just strictly financial, one just strictly legal, and the other one is strictly emotional. It was a telesummit that we did back in 2011, and it's a book plus the audio. That's the sixth book. The seventh book is called *Deep Duty: Living a Spiritual, Emotional and Physical Wellness to your Optimal Health*. That book is not out yet. I've been working on that book for five years on my own. I call myself a guinea pig, because I had to really, really do research, not only as far as looking for research, but trying different things to find out what can I do to get to my optimal health. I discovered many different ways to do all the research. The book will be out hopefully next year.

Kevin: Carolyn, thank you so much for taking the time to chat with us. It's been such a delight to hear your story and your passion, and the way that you fight for seniors. I just wanted to thank you for the price that you've paid to make it safe for seniors as they go forward in their golden years. I really appreciate it. Thank you so much.

Carolyn: Thank you.

CHAPTER 15

Chris Mitchell

Chris Mitchell is the owner of the Mitchell Insurance Agency in Greenwood Village. He represents Farmers Insurance. Chris assists people and business owners with all insurance needs, and he's also licensed in Financial Services, allowing him to work with his clients on retirement planning, college savings plans, employee benefits packages, and other investment needs.

Chris says his background in the restaurant business taught him the importance of serving people properly. He uses that approach with his clients, serving them and their best interests first. His business philosophy is to help people protect the important things in life with insurance, and grow their futures financially.

Kevin: I'm with Chris Mitchell with the Chris Mitchell Insurance Agency. Thanks for taking the time today, Chris.

Chris: Thanks for having me, Kevin.

Kevin: So, tell us a little bit about yourself. Where did you grow up?

Chris: I was born in Greeley, and raised in Littleton, since I was four.

Kevin: What was your childhood like?

Chris: My parents, unfortunately, got divorced when I was 10. My childhood really was spent with years and years on the baseball field, traveling everywhere in competitive baseball.

Kevin: What position?

Chris: I was kind of jack-of-all-trades. You needed me to fill in anywhere, I was your man. But in my prime years, it was mainly catcher and third base.

Kevin: Nice, you got a strong arm. What did your folks do?

Chris: My dad was an entrepreneur. He started his own construction company and went into the truss building business, and then went into code writing. Now, he's a computer consultant. My mom was in technology, the IT side, with the security in technology, firewall protection.

Kevin: So, what made you want to pursue a career in the insurance business?

Chris: It was a total blind leap of faith to tell you the truth. I was doing the restaurant game and had some issues with a new GM, and privileges got taken away. I was starting a family at the time, and getting married. Working nights, weekends and holidays wasn't going to bode well for starting a family and never being able to see the kids, take them to soccer games, whatever it might be. So, I was planning for the future and threw my resume out there, and chance came knocking. I thought, "Well, everybody has to have insurance, right? It's got to be easy." I found out quickly that not everybody likes to switch. I was talking to as many people as I could. Three years down the road now, and I'm still doing it.

Kevin: Yeah, well insurance provides a lot of flexibility for schedules.

Chris: Yeah, that's a definite selling point.

Kevin: So, did you look at other careers or did you just want to sell insurance?

Chris: I had a couple of other sales positions for which I interviewed, and nothing really seemed interesting to me. I never really understood insurance and what it was all about. I did all the classes and licensing. It was pretty interesting stuff. A lot of people have no idea what the benefits are, or the total negatives, or the other side of what insurance can be used for.

Kevin: And you're with a great carrier, too. Farmers is a great company.

Chris: It is definitely a well-known carrier. They have some great products and great prices.

Kevin: What do you wish you had known when you started that you know now?

Chris: How much of a grind it is, really day to day, how many people you need to talk to, what you need to know about, what you have, what you don't have.

Kevin: So, educating people?

Chris: Definitely educating people. I get people in who say they have full coverage, but what does that mean to you? It doesn't mean you are fully covered by anything. That's my favorite response. A lot of times people are just driving around with the state minimums on their cars, so it's just interesting how people can choose coverage without knowing.

Kevin: What kinds of ways do you help seniors as they are in retirement or navigating retirement? You know there's a lot of different issues they have to work through. What specific things do you do to help them?

Chris: Everybody's got a budget. And now that they're in retirement, they're on a stricter budget, so what can we work with? Moneywise, what are their needs? What are their questions? What are their concerns? We develop a plan that fits with what they currently have and what they need? Most of all, you really just put it into a budget.

Kevin: What would you say are the highlights of what you do?

Chris: I would say the highlight is the "aha" moment. When I talk to people, it's like, "Okay, now I understand why I'm paying this monthly bill and what it's doing for me. I've worked my entire life. I've got this money saved up. I've got retirement plans. Now, if I don't have the correct coverages, all that could be taken away in the blink of an eye."

Kevin: One of the big things seniors want to do is age in place. They want to stay at home as long as they can. Is there anything that you do that can make that possible for them?

Chris: I try and get my contacts in touch with a lot of trusted people I work with.

Kevin: You will connect them to some trustworthy people.

Chris: I am connected to trustworthy people that I know do a good job. I personally use these contacts, so I know their work ethic. They are there to really just help.

Kevin: So, Chris, what are some of the most common mistakes you see seniors make as they approach or are in retirement?

Chris: The most common mistake I see is that nobody has explained to them the distribution side of their retirement accounts. They track for years and years how much money they put in, the different avenues they can use to put money into the accounts, but nobody really talks about the distribution and the taxation on those. So again, I just help people. I ask questions like, "What have you been told so far? What questions do you have for me?" Really, I just go through financial matters for them—finding different avenues, keeping their money in longer, and a lot of different products with a lot of different upsides and downsides. I ask what they're really looking for at the age of retirement at 62, or 65, whatever it may be. A lot of people are very worried about it.

Kevin: And they're living longer. They don't know what the quality of life is going to look like, and wonder if they have saved enough.

Chris: They get such a great deal on pension, that they're going to get paid up to the age of 90. Who knows if that pension is going to be there, with that kind of money.

Kevin: What do you like best about your business?

Chris: I like working with people, talking with people. I see different people every day, different needs. Everybody contributes differently. That's why there's no one-size-fits-all for any individual out there. Some people just do quick, "Here you go. Everybody's the same," to just get as many out the door as possible, instead of sitting down and listening to people. Coming from the restaurant business, it's really customer service. People need to understand what they're worried about. That's my theory.

Kevin: What product or technique or service do you offer that you wish more of your senior clients knew about?

Chris: Safe downside protection for their investments. It's not about what you've done at this point, it's about what we can do to show off that money, and keep your paycheck coming in every month. Depending on the vessel and taxation, there are a lot of different areas.

Kevin: Absolutely. Tell about a recent senior client that you helped. What was their situation? What were they hoping to accomplish? And how did you help them?

Chris: The one that comes to mind recently, was actually a client that I picked up through working at the restaurant. A longtime client of mine ended up making friends with her and took over her policies from another agent. That agent wasn't doing her very well, and she had a ton of questions. She said, "Hey, why's my rate so high?" And I said, "It does seem high for your situation. Your husband recently stopped driving, because the doctors told him he couldn't, so let's take a look and see if we can find flexibility in your policy. Let's see where we can put your limits and do all sorts of jumping through hoops that we just talked about." She was comfortable, I was very comfortable, and it ended up getting their bills down a little bit. She was happy about that, obviously, less money coming out.

Kevin: It's tough when you're on a fixed income.

Chris: Yeah, they are very well-off, but we were getting close to being out of their budget. We did a couple of different tweaks and ended up increasing their coverage and saving them very good money.

Kevin: Who's an ideal client for you, Chris?

Chris: An ideal client would be a new family, married, buying a house, somebody that just had a kid and that's maybe looking to have a second kid and moving into their forever home.

Kevin: And what's the first step you'd want your ideal client to take?

Chris: Talk to me.

Kevin: How do these ideal clients find you?

Chris: These ideal clients, they typically don't find me, because we're a-dime-a-dozen. Google "insurance agent near you," and 50 of them will pop up. Some are paying big money for SEO, and others just have a lot of people that truly enjoy their interactions with their agents. So, it's tough for the ideal client to really find me. I have to market to them more directly.

Kevin: So, talk about that, what kind of things do you do to market to ideal clients?

Chris: A lot of social media, actually. I still do old school mailers, phone calls, a lot of events, community activities. Showing people that we're real humans, and trying to put food on our plates like everybody else that's working. We're not just here to take money and give you some sort of shabby policy that you're going to be kicking and screaming and yelling my name when something bad comes up.

Kevin: What's the biggest challenge you're facing right now, Chris?

Chris: The biggest challenge I'm facing is auto rates in Colorado. They're just going up like crazy. The amount of payouts that insurance companies are making are up, due to the uninsured motorist's coverage on people's policies, the number of fatalities that are going on, on the roads right now. More people moving to Colorado.

Kevin: Chris, what's the best advice you've ever received?

Chris: Personally, "Don't quit."

Kevin: That's good advice.

Chris: Another good piece of advice is, "Every ceiling you hit is just another floor to start your next adventure on."

Kevin: What would you like to share that I haven't asked you?

Chris: I'd say insurance-wise, talk to somebody that knows what they're talking about and not just worried about putting money in their pocket. Talk to somebody that's truly in it for their clientele and not just for their bank account.

Kevin: Where can people go to learn more about you?

Chris: They can either search for me on Facebook: Facebook.com/Mitchelladvisors, or call me in my office (720) 399-9909.

Kevin: And you're in Greenwood Village, Colorado.

Chris: The office is in Greenwood Village, but I take care of people throughout the state.

Kevin: Awesome. Thank you.

Chris: Thank you.

CHAPTER 16

Michael Clark

Michael Clark is a director and consulting actuary in P-Solve's Denver office. In his role, he consults on all aspects of financial risk management for defined benefit plans as well as retiree medical plans and defined contribution plans. He also has led numerous clients through pension risk transfers as well as other complex, strategic pension projects. Michael leads P-Solve's business in the West. Prior to joining P-Solve in 2013, Michael worked for Mercer as well as October Three.

Michael is a frequent speaker at industry and professional association conferences on the topics of pension risk management and pension plan administration and has had several articles published in major trade magazines. He currently serves on the Board of Directors for the Conference of Consulting Actuaries as well as the Western Pension & Benefits Council – Denver Chapter.

He is a Fellow of the Society of Actuaries, an Enrolled Actuary, a Fellow of the Conference of Consulting Actuaries, and a Member of the American Academy of Actuaries. Michael graduated magna cum laude from Brigham Young University with a BS in Statistics.

Kevin: I'm with Michael Clark with P-Solve. He's the Director and Consulting Actuary. We'd like to learn a little bit about you, where you're from and all. Where did you grow up?

Michael: I grew up in the Salt Lake City area. I was born and raised there, and went to school out in Utah. After school, I moved to the Denver area about 12 years ago.

Kevin: Decided to upgrade, huh?

Michael: Yeah, absolutely.

Kevin: What was your childhood like?

Michael: It was good. I'm the oldest of eight kids. I have five brothers and two sisters. Half of them are still in Utah, the other half are other places. It was all really good. My father's a used car salesman and owns his own business. My mother was a registered nurse.

Kevin: So was my mom.

Michael: They managed to keep us all busy and out of trouble.

Kevin: That's a lot of kids. Eight kids is a lot of work. So, what made you want to pursue a career as a chief actuary? You mentioned even from high school, you wanted to be an actuary, right?

Michael: Yeah, I did. In fact, during high school I did janitorial work at the Beneficial Life Tower in downtown Salt Lake City. Every once in a while, when we were there late at night doing things, we'd run into the president of the company, Kent Cannon. It turns out his family and my family knew each other, distantly at least. Somebody told me, "You really have to look into what he did." Because before he was president of the company, he was their chief actuary. I had no idea what an actuary was. So, I looked it up, and for me it encompassed a lot of what I was looking for in a career. I still got to be a bit of a math nerd, which I was looking for.

But, in addition to statistics and higher-level math, actuaries have to know economics, have to know accounting, and have to understand some kind of core business principles in finance. Also, in what I do from a consulting perspective, you have to be able to talk to a CFO and HR person, a benefits manager, chief accountants, general counsels, outside counsels and so on—and be able to put these complicated concepts in terms that they can understand and appreciate, to be able to make good decisions.

Kevin: So, you're in a way, a general specialist. You know a lot about a lot, but you're specializing with actuary.

Michael: Yes. That's true.

Kevin: What do you wish you had known when you started, that you now know?

Michael: That's a good question. Like you mentioned, I'm a bit of an oddball. People don't usually stumble on actuarial science until their sophomore or junior years in college. I stumbled on it in high school, and always knew that was what I wanted to do. I've never really thought about that question as it relates to my career, because you kind of gather things along the way.

Kevin: And you really did start pretty early, at least to know what you were after.

Michael: Yes, I did know what I was going after. I always started out in the pension plan side of things. If I had to do it all over again, maybe I would have explored an internship in another area, just for comparison purposes. I did two internships and both were on the pension plan side of things and both with larger companies. I think there would have been some value in checking something else out, just to compare and contrast. Not to say I'm not happy with where my career's gone, just to open up my eyes to more.

Kevin: So, this book is designed for seniors and their kids. What are some ways that you can help seniors?

Michael: One of the things I think is important for seniors to understand is that people are living longer. That's one of the things we study as actuaries. Not to be morbid, but we deal in death, how long people are going to live. And there is a 50 percent chance that one member of a married couple will live past age 90. So, for a lot of couples, especially seniors, being able to manage their retirement is so important. Whether it's through Social Security, their own personal savings, or other means. They have to provide a lifetime income. That's an important concept for seniors to understand.

Kevin: That's pretty new, right? This longevity thing, with medical research and people being healthier and living longer.

Michael: I think people are more cognizant of it, especially over the last 50 years, through advances in medicine and long-term care. Back then, when people got a very debilitating disease, that potentially would have meant the end of life for them. Now there are ways to come back, and they can actually end up still living years down the road. But part of that also means that with long-term care, someone's quality of life might not be the best in their later years.

It can be, but it might not be. When it's not, it can be very, very expensive. So again, making sure there is a financial safety net by way of monthly income is important. That's what Social Security provides. That's what a pension provides. For seniors today, the likelihood that they have a pension benefit is a lot higher than somebody just starting out in the workforce. All of those things are going to contribute to seniors having a predictable lifetime income. It's important. And then supplementing spending with whatever savings they have built up—whether it's through 401(k) plan, their own personal savings and investments, or other things they might have accumulated along the way.

Kevin: So, knowing what you know about statistics and numbers and people living longer and all those kind of things, you just mentioned some specific things, but is there anything else you'd recommend? As a senior is coming to retirement, do they need to prepare for living longer and healthier?

Michael: Yes. In addition to gauging their own hereditary disposition for living long and understanding what that means, understanding what's available to them in Social Security benefits and when is the optimal time to take it is important. If they have other income that they're going to rely on in retirement, it's important to look at what options they have from managing that money to preserve the principle, but still use that money in retirement.

The other thing, and it's something my wife and I have talked about a lot, is people want to leave some sort of inheritance to their children. But I think, because people are living longer, and living longer can be more expensive, one thing that seniors should keep an eye on is not becoming a financial burden to their children. The last thing you want to do is run out of money in your later years, and have to go back to your kids and say, "We need your help." Whether that's, "We need to move in to your basement." A little bit of payback maybe? or "We need help paying for needed medical procedures or prescription drugs."

For example, my wife and I have discussed the fact that our goal for retirement, even though we're still decades away from it, is we don't want to be a financial burden on our children. We want to make sure that from a dad's standpoint and from a retirement-income standpoint, that we can live comfortably and never have to worry about going to our children to say, "We need help."

The other thing we want to avoid is passing away and having obligations that get passed on into the estate that they'll have to deal with. We would much rather not leave them an inheritance, or if we do leave them an inheritance, be something not significant, and be able to take care of ourselves through retirement for however long that could be.

For me, particularly, I tend to have really long longevity on my side. I have grandparents that have lived well into their 90s. So that's a real possibility for us. And again, to the extent that there continue to be medical advances, it's not unfathomable that 10 years from now, somebody will discover a cure for cancer. And that just makes it that much more likely that people are going to live into their 90s—and probably well into their 90s. That's not unfathomable.

Kevin: What would you say are the highlights of your position?

Michael: In terms of what I do as a consulting actuary? We work a lot with companies and with their retirement plans. Anytime we can come in and help a company set up a structure that ultimately means their employees will have a high likelihood of being able to successfully retire, that's satisfying. To be able to do that and do it in the context of the overall enterprise risk management structure of an organization, and be able to help them provide meaningful benefits in that way, that's satisfying for me.

So, for companies that maintain a pension plan, whether that plan is frozen and not growing anymore or still providing ongoing accruals, helping a company successfully manage their plan so that they can make benefit payments into the future is what I enjoy doing. Or for a company with a 401(k) plan, I enjoy helping the company think through the issues—from how much they are going to contribute, in a match or in a profit-sharing contribution, to whether or not they are using the right tools to help employees understand their path through retirement. Making sure that we have all those things in place is satisfying for me.

Kevin: The interesting thing about that is, with these companies that you consult with, you're dealing with the C-level suite. A lot of their employees may never know your company or you. And yet, you're having an impact on their retirement.

Michael: Yes, that's very true. We have very little interactions with the actual people that are benefiting from these retirement plans. We are helping strategically with these retirement plans.

Some of the advances that you and I talked about earlier, 401(k) record keepers are building into their systems. There are some consultants that are helping companies understand the cost of not having their employees be able to retire on time. And there are more companies each year that are taking note of these costs. That helps them focus on the importance of helping their employees become retirement ready. We hope we'll see changes in certain industries, where currently employers might not provide a lot of opportunities for retirement savings or don't contribute employer money to that 401(k) plan. Hopefully they will change their outlook and realize that it's actually more cost-effective to provide those retirement plan dollars, and have them accumulate over time, so that somebody can get it in their 60s and comfortably retire, rather than have that person say, "Oh, I can't retire until I'm in my mid-70s—or later." This becomes very expensive from a disability standpoint, from a time loss standpoint, and from a healthcare standpoint. And all those costs grow with that population, as they get older.

Kevin: Just to summarize what you just said—the more effectively we can plan and prepare for these life events, i.e. retirement, medical costs, etc., the better off we're going to be at our retirement, and the better off our employers will be.

Michael: Exactly.

Kevin: Okay. How did you come to work at P-Solve?

Michael: I've been with P-Solve now for almost four years. I started my career with a big benefits consulting firm called Mercer, part of Marsh & McLennan Companies. I grew up there, but left Mercer after about six years. I went to work for a boutique consulting firm. That firm specialized in retirement plans, but it was using a very specific type of defined benefit pension plan called the Cash Balance Plan. It's a wealth accumulation vehicle. We would set up these plans a lot of times in professional service firms, where you had owners or partners that were maxing out their contributions into their 401(k) plan. If they had the opportunity they would defer even more. So, we set up these plans on top of their 401(k) plan to help them get additional tax-deferred income through a qualified plan vehicle.

Kevin: Was it life insurance, that kind of thing?

Michael: No, it's actually a type of pension plan that they would set up. A qualified plan similar to a 401(k) plan, in the way that it looks and a lot of the ways it behaves. But in a 401(k) plan, for example, between employee and employer contributions you're looking at a maximum amount of $54,000 per year for one person. Add on another $6,000 if you're over 55, for catch-up contributions. But with this type of plan, depending on someone's age, they can put away up to an additional $200,000 a year. So, in some of these professional service firms, like a law firm, maybe somebody's partners are making a lot of money and don't want to spend it all and don't want to have it in separate investments where they're going to get taxed separately. They'd rather be able to put it into a qualified plan where they can get a tax deduction and let that money grow up tax-free. And then, when they retire in their lower income bracket, they can start taking out that money in a much more tax-advantageous way.

Kevin: So, it's almost like a personal pension plan?

Michael: In a way, yes. It depends on the situation. So, I was with that company for two and a half years, and then I got a call from P-Solve. They were looking for somebody to help grow the business out in the West. P-Solve is headquartered in the UK, in London. When I joined, P-Solve was part of an actuarial consulting group called the Punter Southall Group. Their U.S. headquarters is in Boston. They were looking to grow geographically and looking for somebody to help do that. That's right up my alley. It was an opportunity I couldn't pass up, so I joined them.

About a year and a half into the job, Punter Southall spun us off as a separate entity and merged us with an equity manager called River and Mercantile Asset Management, and put that combined entity under the name of River and Mercantile Group. They went public, and so we're actually traded on the London Stock Exchange.

Kevin: That's interesting.

Michael: I love my job. I get to be a numbers geek. I get to consult with clients. I also write a lot of articles, and I speak at a lot of conferences. I have a lot of fun doing all that.

Kevin: You're able to take complex ideas and say, "This is what it means for you." Right?

Michael: That's what we try to do. Yes.

Kevin: That's easier said than done. So, one of the things we hear seniors say, is that they want to stay at home as long as they can. They want to age in place. Again, I know this isn't specifically your target. But is there anything you do to help senior's age in place at home?

Michael: Nothing specific we do. But I think for someone to be able to age in place, it's going to come down to the appropriate financial management of their retirement assets. And a lot of times, that comes back to making sure they have lifetime income. Making sure there's always that steady income source to pay the bills. Whether it's expenses on the house, taxes, insurance, or long-term care, whatever it may be. But making sure that there's a plan in place, such that that money doesn't dry up.

Kevin: As seniors come into retirement or are in retirement, what are some of the common mistakes you see them make?

Michael: There are several things I think people should think through more and not be too quick to make a decision on. One we talked about was when to take Social Security. Some people need that monthly income, and they need it sooner rather than later. But there are a lot of advantages to waiting at least until your full Social Security retirement age. If someone can wait, financially it makes a lot of sense to actually delay your Social Security retirement up to a few years. So, there's that aspect.

The other thing, and this is something that becomes more and more common, especially with seniors that potentially have pension benefits from their employers, is usually you are going to get that monthly paycheck no matter what. But if you've got a pension plan through a corporation, you may have options that would allow you to take that benefit in a lump sum distribution. So instead of getting a monthly check for as long as you live, they're going to come and calculate an actuarial present value of your benefit and give it to you now to manage yourself. Unless you're working as a financial planner and have looked at all your sources for lifetime income, that might not always be the best decision for people to make.

Now, if it's a small amount, you could argue that you're better off taking that lump sum. But, especially when you've got bigger benefits, factoring that into the equation, in terms of lifetime income can be significant and substantial. So, I think that's something that people need to keep their eye on. In the corporate pension plan, one of the things that companies are doing to de-risk their pension plans is actually go out to people and offer them the opportunity to take their benefit as a lump sum in lieu of a monthly annuity benefit.

Studies have shown that people don't always make the best decision when that happens. Because when they do get those offers, it's really hard to say, "I'm going to take $1,000 per month five years from now, as opposed to $200,000 today." That $200,000 today seems like a much better deal. But in the long run, there are trade-offs there in terms of longevity and the stability it can provide people into their retirement years. So, I think it's important to understand and to work with somebody who truly does understand pensions and what those pension promises are—especially if you're given the opportunity to elect your benefit as a lump sum form of payment verses taking it in monthly benefits for the lifetime of you and potentially your spouse.

Because a lot of pension plan sponsors have offered this lump sum form of payments over the years, there's actually a lot of data out there. We did a study a couple years ago where we compiled some data between us and another actuarial firm. It was published in *Pensions & Investments* on the topic of understanding participant behavior in lump sum cash-out windows. So basically, for these people that are given that one-time opportunity to elect their pension benefit in a lump sum, what we saw is that a lot of the people that did take their benefit, would take it in cash. They would get taxed on it immediately as opposed to rolling it over to an IRA or to another 401(k) plan. There's a big difference in what that money is worth if it's taxed today verses taxed at retirement.

Kevin: That's a very good point.

Michael: Here's another tidbit. One of the things we saw is that people that tended to take a lump sum distribution, tended to be the ones that had smaller benefits as opposed to those with larger benefits. But there were still people with larger benefits that would take it.

Kevin: That's a lot of good information. As far as your business, you kind of answered this before, but let's rephrase it a little. What do you like best about your business?

Michael: For me, personally, I like the fact that I'm helping this company grow. I get to wear a business development hat as well as being a technical geek actuary.

Kevin: It's the best of both worlds.

Michael: Yes, I've been able to do a lot of different things. One of the things I appreciate about working for P-Solve is that we're always looking for innovative ways to help companies manage their pension plans. A lot of out-of-the-box solutions. You know one of the things when you think about pension benefits, in particular, when we had the recession in 2008, it really wreaked havoc on pension plans' sponsors. Some plans that were well-funded, all of a sudden found themselves significantly underfunded. And so, we developed some solutions and some thoughts around how companies can really protect themselves from something like that happening. Even if the market does go through some turmoil in the near future, there are things that companies can do from a risk management standpoint. So again, it goes back to, can we help companies comfortably provide those benefits to their employees such that those employees can rest assured that they'll have their retirement dollars at the end of the day?

Kevin: That's awesome. Is there a product or technique or service that you wished more seniors knew about?

Michael: I think we'll see a lot of innovation over the next five to 10 years, especially when you look at the 401(k) plan. 401(k) plans came into being in the 1980s and we've been in an accumulation phase in those types of plans ever since. We're starting to reach this pinnacle where we've got just as much money going out of those plans as we do coming in to those plans. When you've got that happening, you are going to start seeing more product offerings. In fact, we've already seen that. A couple of years ago, we had final regulations for QLACs, which are qualified longevity annuity contracts. These provided a way for people to essentially buy annuities within a qualified plan like a 401(k).

: And since then, we've had a lot of the insurers start developing these QLAC products. What makes those interesting is that you can actually purchase, basically longevity insurance, upfront when you retire, but within the qualified plan structure so that when you come time

| | for your required minimum distributions at age 70 and a half, it doesn't impact those calculations. |

Kevin: That's beautiful.

Michael: It's a really interesting concept. I think you'll start to see more innovation in the decumulation phase. So, I think it's worthwhile for people to work with a financial advisor that understands things like whether it's qualified longevity annuity contracts and qualified plans, or whether it's reverse mortgages as a way to provide lifetime income. For those seniors who are nearing retirement, understanding what type of managed account products are available within a qualified retirement plan. Whether it's a 403(b), 401(k), profit sharing, or whatever. There are professionally managed options that can potentially provide better returns at lower expense ratios. Those are things that I think they should keep an eye on and understand what's out there from a product standpoint, making sure that they've got the ideal situation and have a predictable lifetime income. Monthly income that's coming in month after month for the rest of my life that I can then supplement with whatever other savings or investments that I have. So, having the right mix of those types of assets is something I think seniors should keep an eye on.

Kevin: Really what you're saying is, there's an element of predictability in the world of uncertainty, because there are so many uncertainties surrounding seniors. How long are they going to live? How much money are they going to need? What's the quality of life they're going to have? Those sorts of things. And if we can help them with certainty, we can take away some of that anxiety or pressure.

Michael: That's exactly right.

Kevin: Tell us about a recent client that you worked with. What was the situation? What were you trying to accomplish and how did you help them?

Michael: Let me talk to you about it from the 401(k) plan side of things. Because, in addition to working with pension plans, we work with 401(k) plans. And again, at the company level, rather than the individual level. There have been a lot of advances in technology from record keeper platform standpoints. We've had clients that have been with the same record keepers for years and years and years, and have not seen what's out there. We've had a number of clients over the last couple of years that have wanted to take a look at what else is out there and available. And one of the things we tell them is that they're going to be really impressed by the technology that's been built into these platforms. They've incorporated a lot of behavioral finance components that make it really easy for people to make good decisions.

So, we've helped companies evaluate those different vendors and their capabilities and ultimately select what's going to be best for their employees. And the types of things we're seeing are things like seeing their total balance, as well as what that translates into, in terms of monthly retirement income. And then where the behavioral finance components come in are in things like peer-to-peer comparisons. So, if you can go to somebody and say, "Hey, based on our data, you are in the bottom 10 percent of total contributions. Would you like to get to the 50th percentile? You need to make this change. If you want to make that change, click this button." And clicking that button automatically changes your deferral percentage.

Or it could be something like, "Hey you're not contributing enough to get your employer's match. To take advantage of that, click on this. And this is what it means in terms of the difference in projected lifetime income." So, they're building a lot of these capabilities in, making it easier and easier for people to effortlessly make good decisions that will influence their retirement down the road.

Kevin: What's interesting about that is, somebody can grasp how much $400,000 is. But $2,000 a month, they know exactly what that is.

Michael: That's exactly right. And what a lot of these record-keeping systems have tried to do is to help people understand that. In fact, a few years ago there was a notice of proposed rule-making from the Department of Labor that would actually require plan sponsors of 401(k) plans to issue quarterly statements that actually translate that balance into a lifetime income amount. That's stalled, but I think there's going be some traction to that.

Kevin: That's not a bad idea.

Michael: In the coming years, yes, just to help people understand. But like I said, a lot of the record keepers have actually automatically taken that stage and said, "We're going to build that in anyway, because we think it's useful from a retirement planning standpoint for people to understand."

Kevin: Michael, who is an ideal client for you?

Michael: For us, they're companies that have pension plans. Corporate pension plans are our bread and butter. So. any company that has a pension plan is one that we're going to be well suited for. Or on the 401(k) plan side of things, if it's a middle to large company that has about $20 million in assets in the plan, that's somebody that we can help add value to what they're doing.

Kevin: And what would be the first step you'd like them to take?

Michael: We understand that when you're working with a service provider, there's an element of trust and relationship that has to be built. And we're not blind to that, so we're happy to come in and actually do some high-level projects to help people see how we think about managing retirement plans. The first steps for us are usually to come in and have a conversation, understand what you're trying to do, look under the hood a little bit, and come back with some recommendations. Whether that's the pension plan side of things, "How do we manage this risk to make sure that the plan can remain solid and not be a burden on the company?"

On the 401(k) plan side of things, whether it's making sure they're using the best tools available, making sure they've got a fund line-up that makes sense, and that it is cost-effective. A lot of times what we're seeing, and we see this in litigation, is there are a lot of companies that were sued, because the funds they have in their 401(k) plan are not the most cost-effective. So, the investment management fees can be really expensive.

For the plan itself, based on their size, to actually get lower share classes, would mean they actually pay lower expenses. Paying even a half a percentage point less in investment management fees can mean a significant difference in total retirement income. At the end of the day, being able to come in and look at those things and provide some recommendations and help from the company standpoint, help those fiduciaries that are responsible for those plans carry out their fiduciary duty, and do so in a way that's also meaningful for the company.

Kevin: Currently, how do your ideal clients find you?

Michael: A lot of our work is driven by word of mouth and relationships and referrals. We have a lot of referral partners. Whether they're people that work in the healthcare plan space, because we don't work in that space, attorneys, or even potentially investment partners that are working with companies on their 401(k) plans or their pension plans. Maybe that's not their sole expertise, and they want to bring in a specialist. They will usually come to us, to bring us in on those conversations.

Kevin: How do you market your services to these potential ideal clients to make them aware of you and your company?

Michael: We do quite a bit. We have monthly publications that go out. We have our retirement monthly update that looks at key indicators for pension plan sponsors. We also write a lot of articles. We speak at a lot of conferences. We network with a lot of other service providers that are working in the employee benefit plan and retirement plan arena. That's primarily how we market ourselves.

Kevin: Okay. What's the biggest challenge you're facing right now?

Michael: I would say, rather than speak to this on a company level, I'd speak to it on an industry level. I think we're seeing something akin to what we saw prior to the last recession, which is companies being very complacent with how they're managing their pension plans and their 401(k) plans. Maybe not so much on the 401(k) plans, I think, because there has been plenty of litigation that's forcing people to really take a second look at how their plans are set up and the fund line-ups that they have. And what type of offerings they have and tools that they use.

With pension plans though, prior to the recession, a lot of plans were in really good financial shape. And rather than de-risk their plans, or structure them in a way where the outcomes will be more predictable, they kept rolling the dice. And a lot of plan sponsors lost on that roll when the recession hit. We've seen pension plan funds that have rebounded, but not quite to the levels they were at pre-recession. But with the run-ups in the market over the last seven years, people are starting to ask, "When are we going to see the next market correction?" A lot of people are not necessarily doing everything they can do to make sure they can maintain financially sustainable pension plans.

Kevin: What's the best advice you've ever received?

Michael: I am constantly trying to learn. Whatever it takes to continue to polish around my rough edges. I think for me the best advice has always been, in any kind of relationship, communication is the key. Making sure you can communicate and making sure you're setting realistic expectations, which requires communication. To me, that's some of the best advice I've received from a couple of different channels and that's true whether it's in marriage or in business. Having good communication and open communication, talking about the hard things when you have to talk about the hard things. And celebrating the times when things are good.

Kevin: That sounds great. What would you like to share that I haven't ask you?

Michael: I think we've covered everything I wanted to touch on. But I'll repeat, it's important for people to work with good advisors. That would be number one. Somebody that's going to have your best interest at heart, who can understand your situation and what you're trying to accomplish, and help structure things in way to help meet your goals and objectives. And not everybody's like that. So, it's important that people are looking and making sure that who they're working with really, truly has their best interest. At the forefront, I think a lot of the new fiduciary rules that are coming out will hopefully influence that. Where advisors should be taking on a fiduciary role to make sure that they've got the best interest of their clients at the forefront. And again, they can do that through a variety of ways. Making sure they've got that best interest at heart is probably the most important thing.

Kevin: Where can our readers go to learn more about you and your company?

Michael: Our website which is www.psolve.com. You can read more on some of the things that we're talking to the pension plan sponsors about. Also on LinkedIn. I'm accessible on LinkedIn and even on Twitter. I actually maintain a Twitter account for retirement issues and my handle there is @MichaelClarkFSA. FSA means Fellow of the Society of Actuaries. I can be followed there as well.

Kevin: Awesome. Thank you so much.

Michael: Thank you.

CLOSING THOUGHTS

Thank you for reading this book. I also want to say thank you again to the experts who so graciously agreed to be interviewed, and who shared so much valuable information. I hope you got as much out of reading the interviews as I did conducting them. My goal is for you to use this information, and reach out to these experts for their advice and insights.

Speaking of information, I'd like to wrap things up by sharing some important facts about reverse mortgages. Because, unfortunately, there's a lot of misinformation out there. And in many cases, it's keeping people from even considering applying for a reverse mortgage, and getting the cash flow that can make such a difference in their retirement lifestyle.

So, let's clear up some common myths and misconceptions.

Myth: You lose title to your home
Fact: Homeowners always retain the title to their home, as long as they stay current on property taxes, homeowners' insurance, homeowners' association dues, and any necessary home repairs.

Myth: This is a loan of last resort for people who have no other options
Fact: While many of the people who get reverse mortgages do need the cash flow, many people of means are also obtaining these loans, because they want to put their equity to work for them. They're using the proceeds to buy a vacation home, travel, or other so-called luxury items.

Myth: Eligibility is limited
Fact: You're eligible if at least one of the homeowners is sixty-two

or older, it's their primary residence at least six months of the year, and they have at least fifty percent equity or more.

Myth: You can't leave your home to your children
Fact: The loan comes due when the last homeowner no longer lives in the home. (Death, nursing home, etc.) If there's equity in the home, the heirs sell the house and get the proceeds, or they can refinance and move in to the home. If the home is over leveraged, the borrower or heirs hands the keys over to HUD and walk away as the mortgage insurance makes up any shortfall.

Myth: It will affect taxes and Social Security
Fact: The proceeds from a reverse mortgage are usually tax-free. It is a loan, not income. You are still responsible for property taxes, insurance, and other home-related maintenance. And a reverse mortgage does not affect Social Security or Medicare. Note: this is not tax advice, please consult your advisor.

Myth: Not every type of home is eligible
Fact: The following types of homes are eligible: single-family home, condo, townhouse, two-to-four unit properties, and manufactured homes built after June 1976.

Myth: You have to take the proceeds all at once
Fact: You have these options for taking the proceeds: lump sum, fixed monthly payments for a specific term, monthly payments for as long as you live in the home, a line of credit, or a combination of these options.

Myth: There are limits on how you can use the proceeds
Fact: HUD doesn't care how you spend the money. You can use it to supplement your retirement cash flow to pay for necessities, or use it for lifestyle choices such as a second home. The only restriction is you cannot use it to buy an annuity.

Myth: It's risky

Fact: A reverse mortgage is a very safe loan. Numerous safeguards have been added since the program first began in 1987. Counseling is required, mortgage insurance is required, there are limits on rates and fees, and it's regulated by HUD.

I could go on. But the most important fact I can give you is this: reverse mortgages are safe, and for many senior citizens, this has made a huge difference in their retirement lifestyle. And it would be a shame if the wrong information kept people like you from joining them.

It's not a difficult process, but it can be intimidating. That's why I'm always happy to meet with someone who wants to know more about a reverse mortgage, answer their questions, and help them see how it would work in their specific situation. It's not a sales call. There's never any pressure or obligation. It's really just a chat.

If you'd like to have that type of conversation, maybe over a cup of coffee, call or email me any time. My contact information is below. If you have any questions, I'll answer them for you. You may end up deciding a reverse mortgage isn't the right thing for you. That's fine. I just want to make sure you make the right decision, based on the right information.

Here's to the retirement lifestyle you deserve!

Kevin A. Guttman
Reverse Mortgage Planner
NMLS #384936
877-251-9709
Kevin.Guttman@gmail.com
www.ReverseMortgageRevolution.com

www.ingramcontent.com/pod-product-compliance
Lightning Source LLC
Chambersburg PA
CBHW050201230526
45470CB00001B/193